HOW TO DO THINGS
WITH WORDS

The William James Lectures

delivered at Harvard University

in 1955

J. L. AUSTIN

HOW TO DO THINGS WITH WORDS

Second Edition

Edited by J. O. Urmson
and Marina Sbisà

HARVARD UNIVERSITY PRESS
CAMBRIDGE, MASSACHUSETTS

PREFACE TO THE SECOND EDITION

DR. Sbisà has read through all Austin's notes for these lectures, comparing them with the printed text of the first edition and noting all points at which it seemed to her that improvements could be made. The editors have together examined Austin's notes at all these places and have, as a result, corrected and supplemented the printed text at a number of points. They believe that the new text is clearer, fuller, and, at the same time, more faithful to the actual words of the notes made by Austin. They have added to the appendix a literal transcription of a number of additions made by Austin in the margin or between the lines of his notes, the sense of which was not sufficiently clear for incorporation in the text but which might be of help and interest to the reader.

MARINA SBISÀ
J. O. URMSON

PREFACE TO THE FIRST EDITION

The lectures here printed were delivered by Austin as the William James Lectures at Harvard University in 1955. In a short note, Austin says of the views which underlie these lectures that they 'were formed in 1939. I made use of them in an article on "Other Minds" published in the *Proceedings of the Aristotelian Society*, Supplementary Volume XX (1946), pages 173 ff., and I surfaced rather more of this iceberg shortly afterwards to several societies. . . .' In each of the years 1952–4 Austin delivered lectures at Oxford under the title 'Words and Deeds', each year from a partially rewritten set of notes, each of which covers approximately the same ground as the William James Lectures. For the William James Lectures a new set of notes was again prepared, though sheets of older notes were incorporated here and there; these remain the most recent notes by Austin on the topics covered, though he continued to lecture on 'Words and Deeds' at Oxford from these notes, and while doing so made minor corrections and a number of marginal additions.

The content of these lectures is here reproduced in print as exactly as possible and with the lightest editing. If Austin had published them himself he would certainly have recast them in a form more appropriate to print; he would surely have reduced the recapitulations of previous lectures which occur at the beginning of the second and subsequent lectures; it is equally certain that Austin as a matter of course elaborated on the bare text of his notes when lecturing. But most readers will prefer to have a close approximation to what he is known to have written down rather than what it might be judged that he would have printed or thought that he probably said in lectures; they will not therefore begrudge the price to be paid in minor imperfections of form and style and inconsistencies of vocabulary.

But these lectures as printed do not exactly reproduce Austin's written notes. The reason for this is that while for the most part, and particularly in the earlier part of each lecture, the notes were very full and written as sentences, with only minor omissions such as particles and articles, often at the end of the lecture they became much more fragmentary, while the marginal additions were often very abbreviated. At these points the notes were interpreted and supplemented in the light of remaining portions of the 1952–4 notes already mentioned. A further check was then possible by comparison with notes taken both in America and in England by those who attended the lectures, with the B.B.C. lecture on 'Performative Utterances' and a tape-recording of a lecture entitled 'Performatives' delivered at Gothenberg in October 1959. More thorough indications of the use of these aids are given in an appendix. While it seems possible that in this process of interpretation an occasional sentence may have crept into the text which Austin would have repudiated, it seems very unlikely that at any point the main lines of Austin's thought have been misrepresented.

The editor is grateful to all those who gave assistance by the loan of their notes, and for the gift of the tape-recording. He is especially indebted to Mr. G. J. Warnock, who went through the whole text most thoroughly and saved the editor from numerous mistakes; as a result of this aid the reader has a much improved text.

J. O. URMSON

CONTENTS

LECTURE I

WHAT I shall have to say here is neither difficult nor contentious; the only merit I should
like to claim for it is that of being true, at
least in parts. The phenomenon to be discussed is very
widespread and obvious, and it cannot fail to have been
already noticed, at least here and there, by others. Yet I
have not found attention paid to it specifically.

It was for too long the assumption of philosophers that
the business of a 'statement' can only be to 'describe'
some state of affairs, or to 'state some fact', which it must
do either truly or falsely. Grammarians, indeed, have
regularly pointed out that not all 'sentences' are (used
in making) statements:[1] there are, traditionally, besides
(grammarians') statements, also questions and exclama-
tions, and sentences expressing commands or wishes or
concessions. And doubtless philosophers have not intended to deny this, despite some loose use of 'sentence'
for 'statement'. Doubtless, too, both grammarians and
philosophers have been aware that it is by no means easy
to distinguish even questions, commands, and so on from
statements by means of the few and jejune grammatical
marks available, such as word order, mood, and the like:

[1] It is, of course, not really correct that a sentence ever *is* a statement:
rather, it is *used* in *making a statement*, and the statement itself is a
'logical construction' out of the makings of statements.

though perhaps it has not been usual to dwell on the difficulties which this fact obviously raises. For how do we decide which is which? What are the limits and definitions of each?

But now in recent years, many things which would once have been accepted without question as 'statements' by both philosophers and grammarians have been scrutinized with new care. This scrutiny arose somewhat indirectly—at least in philosophy. First came the view, not always formulated without unfortunate dogmatism, that a statement (of fact) ought to be 'verifiable', and this led to the view that many 'statements' are only what may be called pseudo-statements. First and most obviously, many 'statements' were shown to be, as KANT perhaps first argued systematically, strictly nonsense, despite an unexceptionable grammatical form: and the continual discovery of fresh types of nonsense, unsystematic though their classification and mysterious though their explanation is too often allowed to remain, has done on the whole nothing but good. Yet we, that is, even philosophers, set some limits to the amount of nonsense that we are prepared to admit we talk: so that it was natural to go on to ask, as a second stage, whether many apparent pseudo-statements really set out to be 'statements' at all. It has come to be commonly held that many utterances which look like statements are either not intended at all, or only intended in part, to record or impart straightforward information about the facts: for example, 'ethical propositions' are perhaps intended, solely or partly, to evince emotion or to prescribe conduct or to influence it in special ways. Here too KANT was among the pioneers. We very often also use utterances in ways beyond the scope at least of traditional grammar. It has come to be seen that many specially perplexing words embedded in apparently descriptive statements do not serve to indicate some specially odd additional feature in the reality reported, but to indicate (not to report) the circumstances in which the statement is made or reservations to which it is subject or the way in which it is to be taken and the like. To overlook these possibilities in the way once common is called the 'descriptive' fallacy; but perhaps this is not a good name, as 'descriptive' itself is special. Not all true or false statements are descriptions, and for this reason I prefer to use the word 'Constative'. Along these lines it has by now been shown piecemeal, or at least made to look likely, that many traditional philosophical perplexities have arisen through a mistake—the mistake of taking as straightforward statements of fact utterances which are *either* (in interesting non-grammatical ways) nonsensical *or else* intended as something quite different.

Whatever we may think of any particular one of these views and suggestions, and however much we may deplore the initial confusion into which philosophical doctrine and method have been plunged, it cannot be doubted that they are producing a revolution in philosophy. If anyone wishes to call it the greatest and most salutary in its history, this is not, if you come to think of it, a large claim. It is not surprising that beginnings have been piecemeal, with *parti pris*, and for extraneous aims; this is common with revolutions.

PRELIMINARY ISOLATION OF
THE PERFORMATIVE[1]

The type of utterance we are to consider here is not, of course, in general a type of nonsense; though misuse of it can, as we shall see, engender rather special varieties of 'nonsense'. Rather, it is one of our second class—the masqueraders. But it does not by any means necessarily masquerade as a statement of fact, descriptive or constative. Yet it does quite commonly do so, and that, oddly enough, when it assumes its most explicit form. Grammarians have not, I believe, seen through this 'disguise', and philosophers only at best incidentally.[2] It will be convenient, therefore, to study it first in this misleading form, in order to bring out its characteristics by contrasting them with those of the statement of fact which it apes.

We shall take, then, for our first examples some utterances which can fall into no hitherto recognized *grammatical* category save that of 'statement', which are not nonsense, and which contain none of those verbal danger-signals which philosophers have by now detected or think

[1] Everything said in these sections is provisional, and subject to revision in the light of later sections.

[2] Of all people, jurists should be best aware of the true state of affairs. Perhaps some now are. Yet they will succumb to their own timorous fiction, that a statement of 'the law' is a statement of fact.

they have detected (curious words like 'good' or 'all', suspect auxiliaries like 'ought' or 'can', and dubious constructions like the hypothetical): all will have, as it happens, humdrum verbs in the first person singular present indicative active.[1] Utterances can be found, satisfying these conditions, yet such that

A. they do not 'describe' or 'report' or constate anything at all, are not 'true or false'; and

B. the uttering of the sentence is, or is a part of, the doing of an action, which again would not *normally* be described as, or as 'just', saying something.

This is far from being as paradoxical as it may sound or as I have meanly been trying to make it sound: indeed, the examples now to be given will be disappointing.

Examples:

(E. *a*) 'I do (sc. take this woman to be my lawful wedded wife)'—as uttered in the course of the marriage ceremony.[2]

(E. *b*) 'I name this ship the *Queen Elizabeth*'—as uttered when smashing the bottle against the stem.

(E. *c*) 'I give and bequeath my watch to my brother' —as occurring in a will.

(E. *d*) 'I bet you sixpence it will rain tomorrow.'

[1] Not without design: they are all 'explicit' performatives, and of that prepotent class later called 'exercitives'.

[2] [Austin realized that the expression 'I do' is not used in the marriage ceremony too late to correct his mistake. We have let it remain in the text as it is philosophically unimportant that it is a mistake. J. O. U.]

In these examples it seems clear that to utter the sentence (in, of course, the appropriate circumstances) is not to *describe* my doing of what I should be said in so uttering to be doing[1] or to state that I am doing it: it is to do it. None of the utterances cited is either true or false: I assert this as obvious and do not argue it. It needs argument no more than that 'damn' is not true or false: it may be that the utterance 'serves to inform you'—but that is quite different. To name the ship *is* to say (in the appropriate circumstances) the words 'I name, &c.'. When I say, before the registrar or altar, &c., 'I do', I am not reporting on a marriage: I am indulging in it.

What are we to call a sentence or an utterance of this type?[2] I propose to call it a *performative sentence* or a performative utterance, or, for short, 'a performative'. The term 'performative' will be used in a variety of cognate ways and constructions, much as the term 'imperative' is.[3] The name is derived, of course, from 'perform', the usual verb with the noun 'action': it indicates that the issuing of the utterance is the performing of an action

[1] Still less anything that I have already done or have yet to do.

[2] 'Sentences' form a class of 'utterances', which class is to be defined, so far as I am concerned, grammatically, though I doubt if the definition has yet been given satisfactorily. With performative utterances are contrasted, for example and essentially, 'constative' utterances: to issue a constative utterance (i.e. to utter it with a historical reference) is to make a statement. To issue a performative utterance is, for example, to make a bet. See further below on 'illocutions'.

[3] Formerly I used 'performatory': but 'performative' is to be preferred as shorter, less ugly, more tractable, and more traditional in formation.

—it is not normally thought of as just saying something.

A number of other terms may suggest themselves, each of which would suitably cover this or that wider or narrower class of performatives: for example, many performatives are *contractual* ('I bet') or *declaratory* ('I declare war') utterances. But no term in current use that I know of is nearly wide enough to cover them all. One technical term that comes nearest to what we need is perhaps 'operative', as it is used strictly by lawyers in referring to that part, i.e. those clauses, of an instrument which serves to effect the transaction (conveyance or what not) which is its main object, whereas the rest of the document merely 'recites' the circumstances in which the transaction is to be effected.[1] But 'operative' has other meanings, and indeed is often used nowadays to mean little more than 'important'. I have preferred a new word, to which, though its etymology is not irrelevant, we shall perhaps not be so ready to attach some preconceived meaning.

CAN SAYING MAKE IT SO?

Are we then to say things like this:
'To marry is to say a few words', or
'Betting is simply saying something'?

Such a doctrine sounds odd or even flippant at first, but with sufficient safeguards it may become not odd at all.

---

[1] I owe this observation to Professor H. L. A. Hart.

A sound initial objection to them may be this; and it is not without some importance. In very many cases it is possible to perform an act of exactly the same kind *not* by uttering words, whether written or spoken, but in some other way. For example, I may in some places effect marriage by cohabiting, or I may bet with a totalisator machine by putting a coin in a slot. We should then, perhaps, convert the propositions above, and put it that 'to say a few certain words is to marry' or 'to marry is, in some cases, simply to say a few words' or 'simply to say a certain something is to bet'.

But probably the real reason why such remarks sound dangerous lies in another obvious fact, to which we shall have to revert in detail later, which is this. The uttering of the words is, indeed, usually a, or even *the*, leading incident in the performance of the act (of betting or what not), the performance of which is also the object of the utterance, but it is far from being usually, even if it is ever, the *sole* thing necessary if the act is to be deemed to have been performed. Speaking generally, it is always necessary that the *circumstances* in which the words are uttered should be in some way, or ways, *appropriate*, and it is very commonly necessary that either the speaker himself or other persons should *also* perform certain *other* actions, whether 'physical' or 'mental' actions or even acts of uttering further words. Thus, for naming the ship, it is essential that I should be the person appointed to name her, for (Christian) marrying, it is essential that I should not be already married with a wife living, sane and undivorced, and so on: for a bet to have been made, it is generally necessary for the offer of the bet to have been accepted by a taker (who must have done something, such as to say 'Done'), and it is hardly a gift if I *say* 'I give it you' but never hand it over.

So far, well and good. The action may be performed in ways other than by a performative utterance, and in any case the circumstances, including other actions, must be appropriate. But we may, in objecting, have something totally different, and this time quite mistaken, in mind, especially when we think of some of the more awe-inspiring performatives such as 'I promise to . . . '. Surely the words must be spoken 'seriously' and so as to be taken 'seriously'? This is, though vague, true enough in general—it is an important commonplace in discussing the purport of any utterance whatsoever. I must not be joking, for example, nor writing a poem. But we are apt to have a feeling that their being serious consists in their being uttered as (merely) the outward and visible sign, for convenience or other record or for information, of an inward and spiritual act: from which it is but a short step to go on to believe or to assume without realizing that for many purposes the outward utterance is a description, *true or false*, of the occurrence of the inward performance. The classic expression of this idea is to be found in the *Hippolytus* (l. 612), where Hippolytus says

ἡ γλῶσσ' ὀμώμοχ', ἡ δὲ φρὴν ἀνώμοτος,

i.e. 'my tongue swore to, but my heart (or mind or other

backstage artiste) did not'.[1] Thus 'I promise to . . .' obliges me—puts on record my spiritual assumption of a spiritual shackle.

It is gratifying to observe in this very example how excess of profundity, or rather solemnity, at once paves the way for immodality. For one who says 'promising is not merely a matter of uttering words! It is an inward and spiritual act!' is apt to appear as a solid moralist standing out against a generation of superficial theorizers: we see him as he sees himself, surveying the invisible depths of ethical space, with all the distinction of a specialist in the *sui generis*. Yet he provides Hippolytus with a let-out, the bigamist with an excuse for his 'I do' and the welsher with a defence for his 'I bet'. Accuracy and morality alike are on the side of the plain saying that *our word is our bond*.

If we exclude such fictitious inward acts as this, can we suppose that any of the other things which certainly are normally required to accompany an utterance such as 'I promise that . . .' or 'I do (take this woman . . .)' are in fact described by it, and consequently do by their presence make it true or by their absence make it false? Well, taking the latter first, we shall next consider what we actually do say about the utterance concerned when one or another of its normal concomitants is *absent*. In no case do we say that the utterance was false but rather

---

[1] But I do not mean to rule out all the offstage performers—the lights men, the stage manager, even the prompter; I am objecting only to certain officious understudies, who would duplicate the play.

that the utterance—or rather the *act*,[1] e.g. the promise—
was void, or given in bad faith, or not implemented, or
the like. In the particular case of promising, as with many
other performatives, it is appropriate that the person
uttering the promise should have a certain intention, viz.
here to keep his word: and perhaps of all concomitants
this looks the most suitable to be that which 'I promise'
does describe or record. Do we not actually, when such
intention is absent, speak of a 'false' promise? Yet so to
speak is *not* to say that the utterance 'I promise that . . .'
is false, in the sense that though he states that he does,
he doesn't, or that though he describes he misdescribes—
misreports. For he *does* promise: the promise here is not
even *void*, though it is given *in bad faith*. His utterance
is perhaps misleading, probably deceitful and doubtless
wrong, but it is not a lie or a misstatement. At most we
might make out a case for saying that it implies or
insinuates a falsehood or a misstatement (to the effect
that he does intend to do something): but that is a very
different matter. Moreover, we do not speak of a false
bet or a false christening; and that we *do* speak of a
false promise need commit us no more than the fact that
we speak of a false move. 'False' is not necessarily used of
statements only.

[1] We deliberately avoid distinguishing these, precisely because the
distinction is not in point.

LECTURE II

WE were to consider, you will remember, some cases and senses (only some, Heaven help us!) in which to *say* something is to *do* something; or in which *by* saying or *in* saying something we are doing something. This topic is one development—there are many others—in the recent movement towards questioning an age-old assumption in philosophy—the assumption that to say something, at least in all cases worth considering, i.e. all cases considered, is always and simply to *state* something. This assumption is no doubt unconscious, no doubt is precipitate, but it is wholly natural in philosophy apparently. We must learn to run before we can walk. If we never made mistakes how should we correct them?

I began by drawing your attention, by way of example, to a few simple utterances of the kind known as performatories or performatives. These have on the face of them the look—or at least the grammatical make-up—of 'statements'; but nevertheless they are seen, when more closely inspected, to be, quite plainly, *not* utterances which could be 'true' or 'false'. Yet to be 'true' or 'false' is traditionally the characteristic mark of a statement. One of our examples was, for instance, the utterance 'I do' (take this woman to be my lawful wedded wife), as uttered in the course of a marriage ceremony. Here we should say that in saying these words we are *doing* something—namely, marrying, rather than *reporting* something, namely *that* we are marrying. And the act of marrying, like, say, the act of betting, is at least *preferably* (though still not *accurately*) to be described as *saying certain words*, rather than as performing a different, inward and spiritual, action of which these words are merely the outward and audible sign. That this is so can perhaps hardly be *proved*, but it is, I should claim, a fact.

It is worthy of note that, as I am told, in the American law of evidence, a report of what someone else said is admitted as evidence if what he said is an utterance of our performative kind: because this is regarded as a report not so much of something he *said*, as which it would be hear-say and not admissible as evidence, but rather as something he *did*, an action of his. This coincides very well with our initial feelings about performatives.

So far then we have merely felt the firm ground of prejudice slide away beneath our feet. But now how, as philosophers, are we to proceed? One thing we might go on to do, of course, is to take it all back: another would be to bog, by logical stages, down. But all this must take time. Let us first at least concentrate attention on the little matter already mentioned in passing—this matter of 'the appropriate circumstances'. To bet is not, as I pointed out in passing, merely to utter the words 'I bet, &c.': someone might do that all right, and yet we might still not agree that he had in fact, or at least entirely, succeeded in betting. To satisfy ourselves of this, we have only, for example, to announce our bet after the race is over. Besides the uttering of the words of the so-called performative, a good many other things have as a general rule to be right and to go right if we are to be said to have happily brought off our action. What these are we may hope to discover by looking at and classifying types of case in which something *goes wrong* and the act —marrying, betting, bequeathing, christening, or what not—is therefore at least to some extent a failure: the utterance is then, we may say, not indeed false but in general *unhappy*. And for this reason we call the doctrine of *the things that can be and go wrong* on the occasion of such utterances, the doctrine of the *Infelicities*.

Suppose we try first to state schematically—and I do not wish to claim any sort of finality for this scheme— some at least of the things which are necessary for the smooth or 'happy' functioning of a performative (or at least of a highly developed explicit performative, such as we have hitherto been alone concerned with), and then give examples of infelicities and their effects. I fear, but at the same time of course hope, that these necessary conditions to be satisfied will strike you as obvious.

(A. 1) There must exist an accepted conventional procedure having a certain conventional effect, that
procedure to include the uttering of certain words
by certain persons in certain circumstances, and
further,

(A. 2) the particular persons and circumstances in a given case must be appropriate for the invocation of the particular procedure invoked.

(B. 1) The procedure must be executed by all participants both correctly and

(B. 2) completely.

(*Γ*. 1) Where, as often, the procedure is designed for use by persons having certain thoughts or feelings, or for the inauguration of certain consequential conduct on the part of any participant, then a person participating in and so invoking the procedure must in fact have those thoughts or feelings, and the participants must intend so to conduct themselves,[1] and further

(*Γ*. 2) must actually so conduct themselves subsequently.

Now if we sin against any one (or more) of these six rules, our performative utterance will be (in one way or another) unhappy. But, of course, there are considerable differences between these 'ways' of being unhappy—ways which are intended to be brought out by the letter-numerals selected for each heading.

The first big distinction is between all the four rules A and B taken together, as opposed to the two rules *Γ* (hence the use of Roman as opposed to Greek letters). If we offend against any of the former rules (A's or B's) —that is if we, say, utter the formula incorrectly, or if,

---

[1] It will be explained later why the having of these thoughts, feelings, and intentions is not included as just one among the other 'circumstances' already dealt with in (A).

say, we are not in a position to do the act because we are,
say, married already, or it is the purser and not the
captain who is conducting the ceremony, then the act in
question, e.g. marrying, is not successfully performed at
all, does not come off, is not achieved. Whereas in the
two Γ cases the act *is* achieved, although to achieve it in
such circumstances, as when we are, say, insincere, is an
abuse of the procedure. Thus, when I say 'I promise' and
have no intention of keeping it, I have promised but. . . .
We need names for referring to this general distinction,
so we shall call in general those infelicities A. 1–B. 2
which are such that the act for the performing of which,
and in the performing of which, the verbal formula in
question is designed, is not achieved, by the name
MISFIRES: and on the other hand we may christen those
infelicities where the act *is* achieved ABUSES (do not stress
the normal connotations of these names!) When the
utterance is a misfire, the procedure which we purport to
invoke is disallowed or is botched: and our act (marrying, &c.) is void or without effect, &c. We speak of our
act as a purported act, or perhaps an attempt—or we use
such an expression as 'went through a form of marriage'
by contrast with 'married'. On the other hand, in the Γ
cases, we speak of our infelicitous act as 'professed' or
'hollow' rather than 'purported' or 'empty', and as not
implemented, or not consummated, rather than as void
or without effect. But let me hasten to add that these
distinctions are not hard and fast, and more especially
that such words as 'purported' and 'professed' will not

bear very much stressing. Two final words about being void or without effect. This does not mean, of course, to say that we won't have done anything: lots of things will have been done—we shall most interestingly have committed the act of bigamy—but we shall *not* have done the purported act, viz. marrying. Because despite the name, you do not when bigamous marry twice. (In short, the algebra of marriage is BOOLEAN.) Further, 'without effect' does not here mean 'without consequences, results, effects'.

Next, we must try to make clear the general distinction between the A cases and the B cases, among the misfires. In both of the cases labelled A there is *misinvocation* of a procedure—either because there *is*, speaking vaguely, no such procedure, or because the procedure in question cannot be made to apply in the way attempted. Hence infelicities of this kind A may be called *Misinvocations*. Among them, we may reasonably christen the second sort—where the procedure does exist all right but can't be applied as purported—*Misapplications*. But I have not succeeded in finding a good name for the other, former, class. By contrast with the A cases, the notion of the B cases is rather that the procedure is all right, and it does apply all right, but we muff the execution of the ritual with more or less dire consequences: so B cases as opposed to A cases will be called *Misexecutions* as opposed to Misinvocations: the purported act is *vitiated* by a flaw or hitch in the conduct of the ceremony. The Class B. 1 is that of Flaws, the Class B. 2 that of Hitches.

We get then the following scheme:[1]

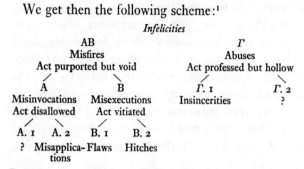

Infelicities

AB — Misfires — Act purported but void

Γ — Abuses — Act professed but hollow

A — Misinvocations — Act disallowed

B — Misexecutions — Act vitiated

Γ. 1 — Insincerities

Γ. 2 — ?

A. 1 — ?

A. 2 — Misapplications

B. 1 — Flaws

B. 2 — Hitches

I expect some doubts will be entertained about A. 1 and Γ. 2; but we will postpone them for detailed consideration shortly.

But before going on to details, let me make some general remarks about these infelicities. We may ask:

(1) To what variety of 'act' does the notion of infelicity apply?

(2) How complete is this classification of infelicity?

(3) Are these classes of infelicity mutually exclusive? Let us take these questions in (that) order.

(1) How widespread is infelicity?

Well, it seems clear in the first place that, although it has excited us (or failed to excite us) in connexion with certain acts which are or are in part acts of *uttering words*, infelicity is an ill to which *all* acts are heir which have

---

[1] [Austin from time to time used other names for the different infelicities. For interest some are here given: A. 1, Non-plays; A. 2, Misplays; B, Miscarriages; B. 1, Misexecutions; B. 2, Non-executions; Γ, Disrespects; Γ. 1, Dissimulations; Γ. 2, Non-fulfilments, Disloyalties, Infractions, Indisciplines, Breaches. J. O. U.]

the general character of ritual or ceremonial, all *conventional* acts: not indeed that *every* ritual is liable to every form of infelicity (but then nor is every performative utterance). This is clear if only from the mere fact that many conventional acts, such as betting or conveyance of property, can be performed in non-verbal ways. The same sorts of rule must be observed in all such conventional procedures—we have only to omit the special reference to verbal utterance in our A. This much is obvious.

But, furthermore, it is worth pointing out—reminding you—how many of the 'acts' which concern the jurist are or include the utterance of performatives, or at any rate are or include the performance of some conventional procedures. And of course you will appreciate that in this way and that writers on jurisprudence have constantly shown themselves aware of the varieties of infelicity and even at times of the peculiarities of the performative utterance. Only the still widespread obsession that the utterances of the law, and utterances used in, say, 'acts in the law', *must* somehow be statements true or false, has prevented many lawyers from getting this whole matter much straighter than we are likely to— and I would not even claim to know whether some of them have not already done so. Of more direct concern to us, however, is to realize that, by the same token, a great many of the acts which fall within the province of Ethics are *not*, as philosophers are too prone to assume, simply in the last resort *physical movements*: very many of them have the general character, in whole or part, of conventional or ritual acts, and are therefore, among other things, exposed to infelicity.

Lastly we may ask—and here I must let some of my cats on the table—does the notion of infelicity apply to utterances *which are statements*? So far we have produced the infelicity as characteristic of the *performative* utterance, which was 'defined' (if we can call it so much) mainly by contrast with the supposedly familiar 'statement'. Yet I will content myself here with pointing out that one of the things that has been happening lately in philosophy is that close attention has been given even to 'statements' which, though not false exactly nor yet 'contradictory', are yet outrageous. For instance, statements which refer to something which does not exist as, for example, 'The present King of France is bald'. There might be a temptation to assimilate this to purporting to bequeath something which you do not own. Is there not a presupposition of existence in each? Is not a statement which refers to something which does not exist not so much false as void? And the more we consider a statement not as a sentence (or proposition) but as an act of speech (out of which the others are logical constructions) the more we are studying the whole thing as an act. Or again, there are obvious similarities between a lie and a false promise. We shall have to return to this matter later.[1]

(2) Our second question was: How complete is this classification?

[1] [See pp. 47 ff. J. O. U.]

(i) Well, the first thing to remember is that, since in uttering our performatives we are undoubtedly in a sound enough sense 'performing actions', then, as actions, these will be subject to certain whole dimensions of unsatisfactoriness to which all actions are subject but which are distinct—or distinguishable—from what we have chosen to discuss as infelicities. I mean that actions in general (not all) are liable, for example, to be done under duress, or by accident, or owing to this or that variety of mistake, say, or otherwise unintentionally. In many such cases we are certainly unwilling to say of some such act simply that it was done or that he did it. I am not going into the general doctrine here: in many such cases we may even say the act was 'void' (or voidable for duress or undue influence) and so forth. Now I suppose some very general high-level doctrine might embrace both what we have called infelicities *and* these other 'unhappy' features of the doing of actions—in our case actions containing a performative utterance—in a single doctrine: but we are not including this kind of unhappiness—we must just remember, though, that features of this sort can and do constantly obtrude into any particular case we are discussing. Features of this sort would normally come under the heading of 'extenuating circumstances' or of 'factors reducing or abrogating the agent's responsibility', and so on.

(ii) Secondly, as *utterances* our performatives are *also* heir to certain other kinds of ill which infect *all* utterances. And these likewise, though again they might be brought into a more general account, we are deliberately at present excluding. I mean, for example, the following: a performative utterance will, for example, be *in a peculiar way* hollow or void if said by an actor on the stage, or if introduced in a poem, or spoken in soliloquy. This applies in a similar manner to any and every utterance—a sea-change in special circumstances. Language in such circumstances is in special ways—intelligibly— used not seriously, but in ways *parasitic* upon its normal use—ways which fall under the doctrine of the *etiolations* of language. All this we are *excluding* from consideration. Our performative utterances, felicitous or not, are to be understood as issued in ordinary circumstances.

(iii) It is partly in order to keep this sort of consideration at least for the present out of it, that I have not here introduced a sort of 'infelicity'—it might really be called such—arising out of 'misunderstanding'. It is obviously necessary that to have promised I must normally

(A) have been *heard* by someone, perhaps the pro-misee;
(B) have been understood by him as promising.

If one or another of these conditions is not satisfied, doubts arise as to whether I have really promised, and it might be held that my act was only attempted or was void. Special precautions are taken in law to avoid this and other infelicities, e.g. in the serving of writs or summonses. This particular very important considera-

tion we shall have to return to later in another connexion.

(3) Are these cases of infelicity mutually exclusive? The
answer to this is obvious.

(*a*) No, in the sense that we can go wrong in two ways
at once (we can insincerely promise a donkey to give it
a carrot).

(*b*) No, more importantly, in the sense that the ways
of going wrong 'shade into one another' and 'overlap',
and the decision between them is 'arbitrary' in various
ways.

Suppose, for example, I see a vessel on the stocks, walk
up and smash the bottle hung at the stem, proclaim 'I
name this ship the *Mr. Stalin*' and for good measure
kick away the chocks: but the trouble is, I was not the
person chosen to name it (whether or not—an additional
complication—*Mr. Stalin* was the destined name; perhaps in a way it is even more of a shame if it was). We
can all agree

(1) that the ship was not thereby named;[1]
(2) that it is an infernal shame.

One could say that I 'went through a form of' naming
the vessel but that my 'action' was 'void' or 'without
effect', because I was not a proper person, had not
the 'capacity', to perform it: but one might also and

[1] Naming babies is even more difficult; we might have the wrong
name and the wrong cleric—that is, someone entitled to name babies
but not intended to name *this* one.

alternatively say that, where there is not even a pretence of capacity or a colourable claim to it, then there is no accepted conventional procedure; it is a mockery, like a marriage with a monkey. Or again one could say that part of the procedure is getting oneself appointed. When the saint baptized the penguins, was this void because the procedure of baptizing is inappropriate to be applied to penguins, or because there is no accepted procedure of baptizing anything except humans? I do not think that these uncertainties matter in theory, though it is pleasant to investigate them and in practice convenient to be ready, as jurists are, with a terminology to cope with them.

LECTURE III

IN our first lecture we isolated in a preliminary way the performative utterance as not, or not merely, saying something but doing something, and as not a true or false report of something. In the second, we pointed out that though it was not ever true or false it still was subject to criticism—could be unhappy, and we listed six of these types of *Infelicity*. Of these, four were such as to make the utterance Misfire, and the act purported to be done null and void, so that it does not take effect; while two, on the contrary, only made the professed act an abuse of the procedure. So then we may seem to have armed ourselves with two shiny new concepts with which to crack the crib of Reality, or as it may be, of Confusion —two new keys in our hands, *and* of course, simultaneously two new skids under our feet. In philosophy, forearmed *should* be forewarned. I then stalled around for some time by discussing some general questions about the concept of the Infelicity, and set it in its general place in a new map of the field. I claimed (1) that it applied to *all* ceremonial acts, not merely verbal ones, and that these are more common than is appreciated; I admitted (2) that our list was *not* complete, and that there are indeed other whole dimensions of what might be reasonably called 'unhappiness' affecting ceremonial performances in general and utterances in general, dimensions which are certainly the concern of philosophers; and (3) that, of course, different infelicities can be combined or can overlap and that it can be more or less an optional matter how we classify some given particular example.

We were next to take some examples of infelicities—of the infringement of our six rules. Let me first remind you of rule A. 1, that there must exist an accepted conventional procedure having a certain conventional effect, that procedure to include the uttering of certain words by certain persons in certain circumstances; and rule A. 2 of course, completing it, was that the particular persons and circumstances in a given case must be appropriate for the invocation of the particular procedure invoked.

A. 1. *There must exist an accepted conventional procedure having a certain conventional effect, the procedure to include the uttering of certain words by certain persons in certain circumstances.*

The latter part, of course, is simply designed to restrict the rule to cases of utterances, and is not important in principle.

Our formulation of this rule contains the two words 'exist' and 'accepted' but we may reasonably ask whether there can be any sense to 'exist' except 'to be accepted', and whether 'be in (general) use' should not be preferred to both. Hence we must not say '(1) exist, (2) be accepted' at any rate. Well, in deference to this reasonable query, let us take just 'accepted' *first*.

If somebody issues a performative utterance, and the utterance is classed as a misfire because the procedure invoked is *not accepted*, it is presumably persons other than the speaker who do not accept it (at least if the speaker is speaking *seriously*). What would be an example? Consider 'I divorce you', said to a wife by her husband in a Christian country, and both being Christians rather than Mohammedans. In this case it might be said, 'nevertheless he has not (successfully) divorced her: we admit only some other verbal or non-verbal procedure'; or even possibly 'we (*we*) do not admit any procedure at all for effecting divorce—marriage is indissoluble'. This may be carried so far that we reject what may be called a *whole code* of procedure, e.g. the code of honour involving duelling: for example, a challenge may be issued by 'my seconds will call on you', which is equivalent to 'I challenge you', and we merely shrug it off. The general position is exploited in the unhappy story of Don Quixote.

Of course, it will be evident that it is comparatively simple if we *never* admit any 'such' procedure at all— that is, any procedure at all for doing that sort of thing, or that procedure *anyway* for doing that particular thing. But equally possible are the cases where we do sometimes —in certain circumstances or at certain hands—accept a procedure, but *not* in any other circumstances or at other hands. And here we may often be in doubt (as in the naming example above) whether an infelicity should be brought into our present class A. 1 or rather into A. 2 (or even B. 1 or B. 2). For example, at a party, you say, when picking sides, 'I pick George': George grunts 'I'm not playing.' Has George been picked? Undoubtedly, the situation is an unhappy one. Well, we may say, you have not picked George, whether because there is no convention that you can pick people who aren't playing or because George in the circumstances is an inappropriate object for the procedure of picking. Or on a desert island you may say to me 'Go and pick up wood'; and I may say 'I don't take orders from you' or 'you're not entitled to give me orders'—I do not take orders from you when you try to 'assert your authority' (which I might fall in with but may not) on a desert island, as opposed to the case when you are the captain on a ship and therefore genuinely have authority.

Now we could say, bringing the case under A. 2 (Misapplication): the procedure—uttering certain words, &c.—was O.K. and accepted, but the circumstances in which it was invoked or the persons who invoked it were wrong: 'I pick' is only in order when the object of the verb is 'a player', and a command is in order only when the subject of the verb is 'a commander' or 'an authority'.

Or again we could say, bringing the case under rule B. 2 (and perhaps we should reduce the former suggestion to this): the procedure has not been completely executed; because it is a necessary *part* of it that, say, the person to be the object of the verb 'I order to . . .' must, by

some previous procedure, tacit or verbal, have first constituted the person who is to do the ordering an authority,
e.g. by saying 'I promise to do what you order me to do.'
This is, of course, *one* of the uncertainties—and a purely
general one really—which underlie the debate when we
discuss in political theory whether there is or is not or
should be a social contract.

It appears to me that it does not matter in principle
at all how we decide in particular cases, though we may
agree, either on the facts or by introducing further definitions, to prefer one solution rather than another. But
neither bringing under A. 2 nor bringing under B will do
as a general rule, and it is important to be clear:

(1) as against B that however much we take into the procedure it would still be possible for someone to reject it *all*;

(2) as against A. 2 that for a procedure to be *accepted*
involves more than for it merely to be the case that it is *in
fact generally used*, even actually by the persons now concerned; and that it must remain in principle open for
anyone to reject any procedure—or code of procedures—
even one that he has already hitherto accepted—as may
happen with, for example, the code of honour. One who
does so is, of course, liable to sanctions; others refuse to
play with him or say that he is not a man of honour.
Above all all must not be put into flat factual circumstances; for this is subject to the old objection to deriving
an 'ought' from an 'is'. (Being accepted is *not* a circumstance in the right sense.) With many procedures, for
example playing games, however appropriate the circum-

stances may be I may still not be playing, and, further, we should contend that in the last resort it is doubtful if 'being accepted' is definable as being 'usually' employed. But this is a more difficult matter.

Now secondly, what could be meant by the suggestion that sometimes a procedure may not even exist—as distinct from the question whether it is accepted, and by this or that group, or not?[1]

(i) We have the case of procedures which 'no longer exist' merely in the sense that though once generally accepted, they are no longer generally accepted, or even accepted by anybody; for example the case of challenging; and

(ii) we have even the case of procedures which someone is initiating. Sometimes he may 'get away with it' like, in football, the man who first picked up the ball and ran. Getting away with things is essential, despite the suspicious terminology. Consider a possible case in which we are more likely to state that the procedure does not exist than that we do not accept it: to say 'you were cowardly' may be to reprimand you or to insult you: and I can make my performance explicit by saying 'I reprimand you', but I cannot do so by saying 'I insult you'—the reasons for this do not matter here.[2] All that

---

[1] If we object here to saying that there is doubt whether it 'exists'—as well we may, for the word gives us currently fashionable creeps which are in general undoubtedly legitimate, we might say that the doubt is rather as to the precise nature or definition or comprehension of the procedure which undoubtedly does exist and *is* accepted.

[2] Many such possible procedures and formulas would be disadvantageous if recognized; for example, perhaps we ought not to allow the

does matter is that a special variety of non-play[1] can arise if someone *does* say 'I insult you': for while insulting is a conventional procedure, and indeed primarily a verbal one, so that in a way we cannot help understanding the procedure that someone who says 'I insult you' is purporting to invoke, yet we are bound to non-play him, not merely because the convention is not accepted, but because we vaguely feel the presence of some bar, the nature of which is not immediately clear, against its ever being accepted.

Much more common, however, will be cases where it is uncertain how far a procedure extends—which cases it covers or which varieties it could be made to cover. It is inherent in the nature of any procedure that the limits of its applicability, and therewith, of course, the 'precise' definition of the procedure, will remain vague. There will always occur difficult or marginal cases where nothing in the previous history of a conventional procedure will decide conclusively whether such a procedure is or is not correctly applied to such a case. Can I baptize a dog, if it is admittedly rational? Or should I be non-played? The law abounds in such difficult decisions—

formula 'I promise you that I'll thrash you'. But I am told that in the hey-day of student duelling in Germany it was the custom for members of one club to march past members of a rival club, each drawn up in file, and then for each to say to his chosen opponent as he passed, quite politely, 'Beleidigung', which means 'I insult you'.

[1] ['Non-play' was at one time Austin's name for the category A. 1 of infelicities. He later rejected it but it remains in his notes at this point. J. O. U.]

in which, of course, it becomes more or less arbitrary whether we regard ourselves as deciding (A. 1) that a convention does not exist or as deciding (A. 2) that the circumstances are not appropriate for the invocation of a convention which undoubtedly does exist: either way, we shall tend to be bound by the 'precedent' we set. Lawyers usually prefer the latter course, as being to apply rather than to make law.

There is, however, a further type of case which may arise, which might be classified in many ways, but which deserves a special mention.

The performative utterances I have taken as examples are all of them highly developed affairs, of the kind that we shall later call *explicit* performatives, by contrast with merely *implicit* performatives. That is to say, they (all) begin with or include some highly significant and un-ambiguous expression such as 'I bet', 'I promise', 'I bequeath'—an expression very commonly also used in naming the act which, in making such an utterance, I am performing—for example betting, promising, bequeath-ing, &c. But, of course, it is both obvious and important that we can on occasion use the utterance 'go' to achieve practically the same as we achieve by the utterance 'I order you to go': and we should say cheerfully in either case, describing subsequently what someone did, that he ordered me to go. It may, however, be uncertain in fact, and, so far as the mere utterance is concerned, is always left uncertain when we use so inexplicit a formula as the mere imperative 'go', whether the utterer is ordering (or is purporting to order) me to go or merely advising, entreating, or what not me to go. Similarly 'There is a bull in the field' may or may not be a warning, for I *might* just be describing the scenery and 'I shall be there' may or may not be a promise. Here we have primitive as distinct from explicit performatives; and there may be nothing in the circumstances by which we can decide whether or not the utterance is performative at all. Anyway, in a given situation it can be open to me to take it as *either* one or the other. It was a performative formula— *perhaps*—but the procedure in question was not sufficiently explicitly invoked. Perhaps I did not *take it as* an order or was not anyway *bound* to take it as an order. The person did not *take it as* a promise: i.e. in the particular circumstance he did not accept the procedure, on the ground that the ritual was incompletely carried out by the original speaker.

We could assimilate this to a faulty or incomplete performance (B. 1 or B. 2): except that it is complete really, though neither unambiguous nor explicit. (In the law, of course, this kind of inexplicit performative *will* normally be brought under B. 1 or B. 2—it is made a rule that to bequeath inexplicitly, for instance, is either an incorrect or an incomplete performance; but in ordinary life there is no such rigidity.) We could also assimilate it to Misunderstandings (which we are not yet considering): but it would be a special kind, concerning the force of the utterance as opposed to its meaning. And the point is

not here just that the audience *did not* understand but
that it did not *have* to understand, e.g. to *take it as* an
order.

We might indeed even assimilate it to A. 2 by saying
that the procedure is not designed for use where it is
not clear that it is being used—which use makes it
altogether void. We might claim that it is only to be
used in circumstances which make it unambiguously
clear that it is being used. But this is a counsel of per-
fection.

A. 2. *The particular persons and circumstances in a given
case must be appropriate for the invocation of the
particular procedure invoked.*

We turn next to infringements of A. 2, the type of
infelicity which we have called Misapplications. Examples
here are legion. 'I appoint you', said when you have
already been appointed, or when someone else has been
appointed, or when I am not entitled to appoint, or
when you are a horse: 'I do', said when you are in the
prohibited degrees of relationship, or before a ship's
captain not at sea: 'I give', said when it is not mine to
give or when it is a pound of my living and non-detached
flesh. We have various special terms for use in different
types of case—'*ultra vires*', 'incapacity', 'not a fit or
proper object (or person, &c.)', 'not entitled', and so on.

The boundary between 'inappropriate persons' and
'inappropriate circumstances' will necessarily not be a
very hard and fast one. Indeed 'circumstances' can

clearly be extended to cover in general 'the natures' of all persons participating. But we must distinguish between cases where the inappropriateness of persons, objects, names, &c., is a matter of 'incapacity' and simpler cases where the object or 'performer' is of the wrong kind or type. This again is a roughish and vanishing distinction, yet not without importance (in, say, the law). Thus we must distinguish the cases of a clergyman baptizing the wrong baby with the right name or baptizing a baby 'Albert' instead of 'Alfred', from those of saying 'I baptize this infant 2704' or 'I promise I will bash your face in' or appointing a horse as Consul. In the latter cases there is something of the wrong kind or type included, whereas in the others the inappropriateness is only a matter of incapacity.

Some overlaps of A. 2 with A. 1 and B. 1 have already been mentioned: perhaps we are more likely to call it a misinvocation (A. 1) if the person *as such* is inappropriate than if it is just because it is not the duly appointed one (A. 2)—if *nothing*—no antecedent procedure or appointment, &c.—could have put the matter in order. On the other hand, if we take the question of *appointment* literally (position as opposed to status) we might class the infelicity as a matter of wrongly executed (B. 1) rather than as misapplied procedure—for example, if we vote for a candidate before he has been nominated. The question here is how far we are to go back in the 'procedure'.

Next we have examples of B (already, of course, trenched upon) called Misexecutions.

B. 1. *The procedure must be executed by all participants correctly.*

These are flaws. They consist in the use of, for example, wrong formulas—there is a procedure which is appropriate to the persons and the circumstances, but it is not gone through correctly. Examples are more easily seen in the law; they are naturally not so definite in ordinary life, where allowances are made. The use of inexplicit formulas might be put under this heading. Also under this heading falls the use of vague formulas and uncertain references, for example if I say 'my house' when I have two, or if I say 'I bet you the race won't be run today' when more than one race was arranged.

This is a different question from that of misunderstanding or slow up-take by the audience; a flaw in the ritual is involved, however the audience took it. One of the things that cause particular difficulty is the question whether when two parties are involved '*consensus ad idem*' is necessary. Is it essential for me to secure *correct understanding* as well as everything else? In any case this is clearly a matter falling under the B rules and not under the Γ rules.

B. 2. *The procedure must be executed by all participants completely.*

These are hitches; we attempt to carry out the procedure but the act is abortive. For example: my attempt to make a bet by saying 'I bet you sixpence' is abortive unless you say 'I take you on' or words to that effect; my attempt to marry by saying 'I will' is abortive if the woman says 'I will not'; my attempt to challenge you is abortive if I say 'I challenge you' but I fail to send round my seconds; my attempt ceremonially to open a library is abortive if I say 'I open this library' but the key snaps in the lock; conversely the christening of a ship is abortive if I kick away the chocks before I have said 'I launch this ship'. Here again, in ordinary life, a certain laxness in procedure is permitted—otherwise no university business would ever get done!

Naturally sometimes uncertainties about whether anything further is required or not will arise. For example, are you required to accept the gift if I am to give you something? Certainly in formal business acceptance is required, but is this ordinarily so? Similar uncertainty arises if an appointment is made without the consent of the person appointed. The question here is how far can acts be unilateral? Similarly the question arises as to when the act is at an end, what counts as its completion?[1]

In all this I would remind you that we were *not* invoking such further dimensions of unhappiness as may arise from, say, the performer making a simple mistake of fact or from disagreements over matters of fact, let alone disagreements of opinion; for example, there is no convention that I can promise you to do something to your detriment, thus putting myself under an obligation to

---

[1] It might thus be doubted whether failure to hand a gift over is a failure to complete the gift or an infelicity of type Γ.

you to do it; but suppose I say 'I promise to send you to a nunnery'—when I think, but you do not, that this will be for your good, or again when you think it will but I do not, or even when we both think it will, but in fact, as may transpire, it will not? Have I invoked a non-existent convention in inappropriate circumstances? Needless to say, and as a matter of general principle, there can be no satisfactory choice between these alternatives, which are too unsubtle to fit subtle cases. There is no short cut to expounding simply the full complexity of the situation which does not exactly fit any common classification.

It may appear in all this that we have merely been taking back our rules. But this is not the case. Clearly there are these six possibilities of infelicity even if it is sometimes uncertain which is involved in a particular case: and we *might* define them, at least for given cases, if we wished. And we must at all costs avoid over-simplification, which one might be tempted to call the occupational disease of philosophers if it were not their occupation.

LECTURE IV

LAST time we were considering cases of Infelicities: and we dealt with cases where there was no procedure or no accepted procedure: where the procedure was invoked in inappropriate circumstances; and where the procedure was faultily executed or incompletely executed. And we pointed out that in particular cases these can be made to overlap; and that they generally overlap with (*a*) Misunderstandings, a type of infelicity to which all utterances are probably liable, and (*b*) Mistakes, and acting under duress.

The last type of case is that of Γ. 1 and Γ. 2, insincerities and infractions or breaches.[1] Here, we say, the performance is *not* void, although it is still unhappy.

Let me repeat the definitions:

Γ. 1: where, as often, the procedure is designed for use by persons having certain thoughts, feelings, or intentions, or for the inauguration of certain consequential conduct on the part of any participant, then a person participating in and so invoking the procedure must in fact have those thoughts, feelings, or intentions, and the participants must intend so to conduct themselves;

Γ. 2: and the participants must so conduct themselves subsequently.

[1] See p. 18 and footnote.

1. *Feelings*

Examples of not having the requisite feelings are:

'I congratulate you', said when I did not feel at all pleased, perhaps even was annoyed.

'I condole with you', said when I did not really sympathize with you.

The circumstances here are in order and the act is performed, not void, but it is actually *insincere*; I had no business to congratulate you or to condole with you, feeling as I did.

2. *Thoughts*

Examples of not having the requisite thoughts are:

'I advise you to', said when I do not think it would be the course most expedient for you.

'I find him not guilty—I acquit', said when I do believe that he was guilty.

These acts are not void. I do advise and bring a verdict, though insincerely. Here there is an obvious parallel with one element in *lying*, in performing a speech-act of an *assertive* kind.

3. *Intentions*

Examples of not having the requisite intentions are:

'I promise', said when I do not intend to do what I promise.

'I bet', said when I do not intend to pay.

'I declare war', said when I do not intend to fight.

I am not using the terms 'feelings', 'thoughts', and 'intentions' in a technical as opposed to a loose way. But some comments are necessary:

(1) The distinctions are so loose that the cases are not necessarily easily distinguishable: and anyway, of course, the cases can be combined and usually are combined. For example, if I say 'I congratulate you', must we really have a feeling or rather a thought that you have done or deserved well? Have I a thought or a feeling that it was highly creditable? Or again in the case of promising I must certainly intend: but I must also think what I promise feasible (must intend to do it, not merely to try to do it) and think perhaps that the promisee thinks it to be to his advantage, or think that it is to his advantage.

(2) In the case of thoughts we must distinguish really thinking it to be so—for example that he was guilty, that the deed was done by him, or that the credit was his, the feat was performed by him—from what we think to be so really being so, the thought being correct as opposed to mistaken. (Similarly, we can distinguish really feeling so from what we feel being justified, and really intending to from what we intend being feasible.) But thoughts are a most interesting, i.e. a confusing, case: there is insincerity here which is an essential element in lying as distinct from merely saying what is in fact false. Examples are thinking when I say 'not guilty' that the deed was done by him, or thinking when I say 'I congratulate' that the feat was not performed by him. But I may in fact be mistaken in so thinking.

If some at least of our thoughts are incorrect (as opposed to insincere), this may result in an infelicity of course of a different kind:

(*a*) I may give something which is not in fact (though I think it is) mine to give. We might say that this is 'Misapplication', that the circumstances, objects, persons, &c., are not appropriate for the procedure of giving. But we must remember that we said that we would rule out the whole dimension of what might well be called Infelicity but which arose from mistake and misunderstanding. It should be noted that mistake will not in general make an act *void*, though it may make it *excusable*.

(*b*) 'I advise you to do X' is a performative utterance; consider the case of my advising you to do something which is not in fact at all in your interest, though I think it is. This case is quite different from (*a*) in that here there is no temptation at all to think that the act of advising might be perhaps void or voidable, and likewise there is no temptation to think it insincere. Rather we here introduce an entirely new dimension of criticism again; we would criticize this as *bad* advice. In many ways this is the worst thing one can say about advice. That an act is happy or felicitous in all our ways does not exempt it from all criticism. We shall come back to this.

(*c*) More difficult than either of these cases is one to which we shall also return later. There is a class of performatives which I call *verdictives*: for example, when we say 'I find the accused guilty' or merely 'guilty', or when the umpire says 'out'. When we say 'guilty', this is happy in a way if we sincerely think on the evidence that he did it. *But*, of course, the whole point of the procedure in a way is to be correct; it may even be scarcely a matter of opinion, as above. Thus when the umpire says 'over', this terminates the over. But again we may have a 'bad' verdict: it may either be *unjustified* (jury) or even *incorrect* (umpire). So here we have a very unhappy situation. But still it is *not* infelicitous in any of our senses: it is not void (if the umpire says 'out', the batsman is out; the umpire's decision is final) and not insincere. However, we are not concerned now with these impending troubles but only to distinguish insincerity.

(3) In the case of intention too there are certain special awkwardnesses:

(*a*) We have already noticed the dubiety about what constitutes a subsequent action and what is merely the completion or consummation of the one, single, total action: for example, it is hard to determine the relation between

'I give' and surrendering possession,
'I do' (take this woman &c.) and consummation.
'I sell' and completion of sale:

though the distinction is easy in the case of promising. So there are similar possibilities of drawing distinctions in different ways over what is the requisite intention of performing a *subsequent* action and what is the requisite intention to complete the *present* action. This does not raise any trouble in principle, however, about the concept of insincerity.

(*b*) We have distinguished roughly cases where you must have certain intentions from more particular cases where you must intend to carry out a certain further course of action, where use of the given procedure was precisely designed to inaugurate it (whether making it obligatory or permissive). Instances of this more specialized procedure are undertaking to perform an action, of course, and probably also christening. The whole point of having such a procedure is precisely to make certain subsequent conduct in order and other conduct out of order: and of course for many purposes, with, for example, legal formulas, this goal is more and more nearly approached. But other cases are not so easy: I may, for example, express my intention simply by saying 'I shall. . .'. I must, of course, have the intention, if I am not to be insincere, at the time of my utterance: but what exactly is the degree or mode of the infelicity if I do not afterwards do it? Or again, in 'I bid you welcome', to say which is to welcome, intentions of a kind are presumably vaguely necessary: but what if one then behaves churlishly? Or again, I give you advice and you accept it, but then I round on you: how far is it obligatory on me not to do so? Or am I just 'not expected' to do so?: or is part of asking-and-taking advice definitely to make such subsequent conduct out of order? Or similarly, I entreat you to do something, you accede, and then I protest—am I out of order? Probably yes. But there is a constant tendency to make this sort of thing clearer, as for example, when we move from 'I forgive' to 'I pardon' or from 'I will' either to 'I intend' or to 'I promise'.

So much then for ways in which performative utterances can be unhappy, with the result that the 'act' concerned is merely purported or professed, &c. Now in general this amounted to saying, if you prefer jargon, that certain conditions have to be satisfied if the utterance is to be happy—certain things have to be so. And this, it seems clear, commits us to saying that for a certain performative utterance to be happy, certain statements have *to be true*. This in itself is no doubt a very trivial result of our investigations. Well, to avoid at least the infelicities that we have considered,

(1) what are these statements that have to be true? and
(2) can we say anything exciting about the relation of the performative utterance to them?

Remember that we said in the first Lecture that we might in some sense or way *imply* lots of things to be so when we say 'I promise', but this is completely different from saying that the utterance, 'I promise', is a *statement*, true or false, that these things are so. I shall take some important things which must be true if the performance is to be happy (not all—but even these will now seem boring and trivial enough: I hope so, for that will mean 'obvious' *by now*).

Now if when, for example, I say 'I apologize' I do

apologize, so that we can now say, I or he did definitely apologize, then

(1) it is true and not false that I am doing (have done) something—actually numerous things, but in particular that I am apologizing (have apologized);

(2) it is true and not false that certain conditions do obtain, in particular those of the kind specified in our Rules A. 1 and A. 2;

(3) it is true and not false that certain other conditions obtain of our kind Γ, in particular that I am thinking something; and

(4) it is true and not false that I am committed to doing something subsequently.

Now strictly speaking and importantly, the sense in which 'I apologize' implies the truth of each one of these has already been explained—we have been explaining this very thing. But what is of interest is to compare these 'implications' of performative utterances with certain discoveries made comparatively recently about the 'implications' of the contrasted and preferred type of utterance, the *statement* or constative utterance, which itself, unlike the performative, is true or false.

First to take (1): what is the relation between the utterance, 'I apologize', and the fact that I am apologizing? It is important to see that this is different from the relation between 'I am running' and the fact that I am running (or in case that is not a genuine 'mere' report—between 'he is running' and the fact that he is running).

This difference is marked in English by the use of the non-continuous present in performative formulas: it is not, however, necessarily marked in all languages—which may lack a continuous present—or even always in English.

We might say: in ordinary cases, for example running, it is the fact that he is running which makes the statement that he is running *true*; or again, that the truth of the constative utterance 'he is running' depends on his being running. Whereas in our case it is the happiness of the performative 'I apologize' which makes it the fact that I am apologizing: and my success in apologizing depends on the happiness of the performative utterance 'I apologize'. This is one way in which we might justify the 'performative-constative' distinction—as a distinction between doing and saying.

We shall next consider three of the many ways in which a statement implies the truth of certain other statements. One of those that I shall mention has been long known. The others have been discovered quite recently. We shall not put the matter too technically, though this can be done. I refer to the discovery that the ways we can do wrong, speak outrageously, in uttering conjunctions of 'factual' statements, are more numerous than merely by contradiction (which anyway is a complicated relation which requires and could be given both definition and explanation).

1. *Entails*

'All men blush' entails 'some men blush'. We cannot

say 'All men blush but not any men blush', or 'the cat is under the mat and the cat is on top of the mat' or 'the cat is on the mat and the cat is not on the mat', since in each case the first clause entails the contradictory of the second.

2. *Implies*

My saying 'the cat is on the mat' implies that I believe it is, in a sense of 'implies' just noticed by G. E. Moore. We cannot say 'the cat is on the mat but I do not believe it is'. (This is actually not the ordinary use of 'implies': 'implies' is really weaker: as when we say 'He implied that I did not know it' or 'You implied you knew it (as distinct from believing it)'.)

3. *Presupposes*

'All Jack's children are bald' presupposes that Jack has some children. We cannot say 'All Jack's children are bald but Jack has no children', or 'Jack has no children and all his children are bald'.

There is a common feeling of outrage in all these cases. But we must not use some blanket term, 'implies' or 'contradiction', because there are very great differences. There are more ways of killing a cat than drowning it in butter; but this is the sort of thing (as the proverb indicates) we overlook: there are more ways of outraging speech than contradiction merely. The major questions are: how many ways, and why they outrage speech, and wherein the outrage lies?

Let us contrast the three cases in familiar ways:

1. *Entails*

If p entails q then $\sim q$ entails $\sim p$: if 'the cat is on the mat' entails 'the mat is under the cat' then 'the mat is not under the cat' entails 'the cat is not on the mat'. Here the truth of a proposition entails the truth of a further proposition or the truth of one is inconsistent with the truth of another.

2. *Implies*

This is different: if my saying that the cat is on the mat implies that I believe it to be so, it is not the case that my not believing that the cat is on the mat implies that the cat is not on the mat (in ordinary English). And again, we are not concerned here with the inconsistency of propositions: they are perfectly compatible: it may be the case at once that the cat is on the mat but I do not believe that it is. But we cannot in the other case say 'it may be the case at once that the cat is on the mat but the mat is not under the cat'. Or again, here it is saying that 'the cat is on the mat', which is not possible along with saying 'I do not believe that it is'; the assertion implies a belief.

3. *Presupposes*

This again is unlike entailment: if 'John's children are bald' presupposes that John has children, it is not true that John's having no children presupposes that John's children are not bald. Moreover again, *both* 'John's children are bald' and 'John's children are not bald' alike presuppose that John has children: but it is not the case that both 'the cat is on the mat' and 'the cat is not on the mat' alike entail that the cat is below the mat.

Let us consider first 'implies' and then 'presupposes' over again:

Implies

Suppose I did say 'the cat is on the mat' when it is not the case that I believe that the cat is on the mat, what should we say? Clearly it is a case of *insincerity*. In other words: the unhappiness here is, though affecting a statement, exactly the same as the unhappiness infecting 'I promise . . .' when I do not intend, do not believe, &c. The insincerity of an assertion is the same as the insincerity of a promise, since both promising and asserting are procedures intended for use by persons having certain thoughts. 'I promise but do not intend' is parallel to 'it is the case but I do not believe it'; to say 'I promise', without intending, is parallel to saying 'it is the case' without believing.

Presupposition

Next let us consider presupposition: what is to be said of the statement that 'John's children are all bald' if made when John has no children? It is usual now to say that it is *not* false because it is devoid of reference; reference is necessary for either truth or falsehood. (Is it then meaningless? It is not so in every sense: it is not, like a 'meaningless sentence', ungrammatical, incomplete, mumbo-jumbo, &c.) People say 'the question does not arise'. Here I shall say 'the utterance is void'.

Compare this with our infelicity when we say 'I name . . .', but some of the conditions (A. 1) and (A. 2) are not satisfied (specially A. 2 perhaps, but really equally—a parallel presupposition to A. 1 exists with statements also!). Here we might have used the 'presuppose' formula: we might say that the formula 'I do' presupposes lots of things: if these are not satisfied the formula is unhappy, void: it does not succeed in being a contract when the reference fails (or even when it is ambiguous) any more than the other succeeds in being a statement. Similarly the question of goodness or badness of advice does not arise if you are not in a position to advise me about that matter.

Lastly, it might be that the way in which in entailment one proposition entails another is not unlike the way 'I promise' entails 'I ought': it is not the same, but it is parallel: 'I promise but I ought not' is parallel to 'it is and it is not'; to say 'I promise' but not to perform the act is parallel to saying both 'it is' and 'it is not'. Just as the purpose of assertion is defeated by an internal contradiction (in which we assimilate and contrast *at once* and so stultify the whole procedure), the purpose of a contract is defeated if we say 'I promise and I ought not'. This commits you to it and refuses to commit you to it. It is a self-stultifying procedure. One assertion commits us to another assertion, one performance to another performance. Moreover, just as if p entails q then $\sim q$ entails $\sim p$, so 'I ought not' entails 'I do not promise'.

In conclusion, we see that in order to explain what can go wrong with statements we cannot just concentrate on the proposition involved (whatever that is) as has been done traditionally. We must consider the total situation in which the utterance is issued—the total speech-act—if we are to see the parallel between statements and performative utterances, and how each can go wrong. So the total speech act in the total speech situation is emerging from logic piecemeal as important in special cases: and thus we are assimilating the supposed constative utterance to the performative.

LECTURE V

AT the end of the previous lecture we were reconsidering the question of the relations between the performative utterance and statements of various kinds which certainly are true or false. We mentioned as specially notable four such connexions:

(1) If the performative utterance 'I apologize' is happy, then the statement that I am apologizing is true.

(2) If the performative utterance 'I apologize' is to be happy, then the statement that certain conditions obtain —those notably in Rules A. 1 and A. 2—must be true.

(3) If the performative utterance 'I apologize' is to be happy, then the statement that certain other conditions obtain—those notably in our rule Γ. 1—must be true.

(4) If performative utterances of at least some kinds are happy, for example contractual ones, then statements typically of the form that I ought or ought not subsequently to do some particular thing are true.

I was saying that there seemed to be some similarity, and perhaps even an identity, between the second of these connexions and the phenomenon which has been called, in the case of statements as opposed to performatives, 'presupposition': and likewise between the third of these connexions and the phenomenon called (sometimes and not, to my mind, correctly) in the case of statements, 'implication'; these, presupposition and implication, being two ways in which the truth of a statement may be connected importantly with the truth of another without it being the case that the one entails the other in the sole sort of sense preferred by obsessional logicians. Only the fourth and last of the above connexions could be made out—I do not say how satisfactorily—to resemble entailment between statements. 'I promise to do X but I am under no obligation to do it' may certainly look more like a self-contradiction—whatever that is—than 'I promise to do X but I do not intend to do it': also 'I am under no obligation to do p' might be held to entail 'I did not promise to do p', and one might think that the way in which asserting p commits me to asserting q is not unlike the way in which promising to do X commits me to doing X. But I do not want to say that there is or is not any parallel here; only that at least there is a very close parallel in the other two cases; which suggest that at least in some ways there is danger of our initial and tentative distinction between constative and performative utterances breaking down.

We may, however, fortify ourselves in the conviction that the distinction is a final one by reverting to the old idea that the constative utterance is true or false and the performative is happy or unhappy. Contrast the fact that I am apologizing, which depends on the performative 'I apologize' being happy, with the case of the statement 'John is running', which depends for its truth on its being the fact or case that John is running. But perhaps this contrast is not so sound either: for, to take statements first, connected with the utterance (constative) 'John is running' is the statement 'I am stating that John is running': and this may depend for its truth on the happiness of 'John is running', just as the truth of 'I am apologizing' depends on the happiness of 'I apologize'. And, to take performatives second: connected with the performative (I presume it is one) 'I warn you that the bull is about to charge' is the fact, if it is one, that the bull is about to charge: if the bull is *not*, then indeed the utterance 'I warn you that the bull is about to charge' is open to criticism—but not in any of the ways we have hitherto characterized as varieties of unhappiness. We should not in this case say the warning was void—i.e. that he did not warn but only went through a form of warning—nor that it was insincere: we should feel much more inclined to say the warning was false or (better) mistaken, as with a statement. So that considerations of the happiness and unhappiness type may infect statements (or some statements) and considerations of the type of truth and falsity may infect performatives (or some performatives).

We have then to take a further step out into the desert of comparative precision. We must ask: is there some precise way in which we can definitely distinguish the performative from the constative utterance? And in particular we should naturally ask first whether there is some *grammatical* (or lexicographical) criterion for distinguishing the performative utterance.

So far we have considered only a small number of classic examples of performatives, all with verbs in the first person singular present indicative active. We shall see very shortly that there were good reasons for this piece of slyness. Examples are 'I name', 'I do', 'I bet', 'I give'. There are fairly obvious reasons, with which I shall nevertheless shortly deal, why this is the commonest type of explicit performative. Note that 'present' and 'indicative' are, of course, both misnomers (not to mention the misleading implications of 'active')—I am only using them in the well-known grammatical way. For example the 'present', as distinct from 'continous present', is normally nothing to do with describing (or even indicating) what I am doing at present. 'I drink beer', as distinct from 'I am drinking beer', is not analogous to a future and a past tense describing what I shall do in the future or have done in the past. It is really more commonly the *habitual* indicative, when it is 'indicative' at all. And where it is not habitual but in a way 'present' genuinely, as in a way it is in performatives, if you like, such as 'I name', then it is certainly not 'indicative' in the sense grammarians intend, that is reporting, describing, or informing about an actual state of affairs or occurrent event: because, as we have seen, it does not describe or inform at all, but is used for, or in, the doing of something. So we use 'present indicative' merely to mean the English grammatical form 'I name', 'I run', &c. (This mistake in terminology is due to assimilating, for example, 'I run' to the Latin *curro*, which should really generally be translated 'I am running'; Latin does not have two tenses where we do.)

Well, is the use of the first person singular and of the present indicative active, so called, essential to a performative utterance? We need not waste our time on the obvious exception of the first person plural, '*we* promise . . .', 'we consent', &c. There are more important and obvious exceptions all over the place (some of which have already been alluded to in passing).

A very common and important type of, one would think, indubitable performative has the verb in the *second or third person* (singular or plural) and the verb in the *passive* voice: so person and voice anyway are not essential. Some examples of this type are:

(1) You are hereby authorized to pay . . . .
(2) Passengers are warned to cross the track by the bridge only.

Indeed the verb may even be 'impersonal' in such cases with the passive, for example:

(3) Notice is hereby given that trespassers will be prosecuted.

This type is usually found on formal or legal occasions; and it is characteristic of it that, in writing at least, the word 'hereby' is often and perhaps can always be inserted; this serves to indicate that the utterance (in writing) of the sentence is, as it is said, the instrument effecting the act of warning, authorizing, &c. 'Hereby' is a useful criterion that the utterance is performative. If it is not put in, 'passengers are . . .' may be used for the description of what usually happens; as for example in 'on nearing the tunnel, passengers are warned to duck their heads, &c.'

However, if we turn away from these highly formalized and explicit performative utterances, we have to recognize that mood and tense (hitherto retained as opposed to person and voice) break down as absolute criteria.

Mood (whatever this may be in English as opposed to Latin) will not do, for I may order you to turn right by saying, not 'I order you to turn right', but simply 'Turn right'; I may give you permission to go by saying simply 'You may go'; and instead of 'I advise [or "recommend"] you to turn right' I may say 'I should turn to the right if I were you'. Tense will not do either, for in giving (or calling) you off-side I may say, instead of 'I give [or "call"] you off-side', simply 'You were off-side'; and similarly, instead of saying 'I find you guilty' I may just say 'You did it'. Not to mention cases where we have only a truncated sentence, as when I accept a bet by saying simply 'Done', and even cases where there is no explicit verb at all, as when I say simply 'Guilty' in finding a person guilty, or 'Out' to give someone out.

Particularly with some special performative-looking words, for example 'off-side', 'liable', &c., we seem able to refute even the rule governing the use of the active or passive which we gave above. Instead of 'I pronounce you off-side' I might say 'You are off-side' and I might say 'I am (hereby rendered) liable' instead of 'I undertake . . .'. So we might think certain *words* might do as a test of the performative utterance, that we could do it by means of *vocabulary* as distinct from *grammar*. Such words might be 'off-side', 'authorized', 'promise', 'dangerous', &c. But this will not do, for:

I. We may get the performative without the operative words thus:

(1) In place of 'dangerous corner' we may have 'corner', and in place of 'dangerous bull' we may write 'bull'.

(2) In place of 'you are ordered to . . .', we may have 'you will', and in place of 'I promise to . . .' we may have 'I shall'.

II. We may get the operative word without the utterance being performative, thus:

(1) In cricket a spectator may say 'it was over (really)'. Similarly I may say 'you were guilty' or 'you were off-side' or even 'you are guilty (off-side)' when I have no right to pronounce you guilty or off-side.

(2) In such locutions as 'you promised', 'you authorize' &c., the word occurs in a non-performative use.

This reduces us to an impasse over any *single simple* criterion of grammar or vocabulary. But maybe it is not impossible to produce a complex criterion, or at least a set of criteria, simple or complex, involving both grammar and vocabulary. For example, one of the criteria might be that everything with the verb in the imperative mood is performative (this leads, however, to many troubles over, for example, when a verb is in the imperative mood and when it is not, into which I do not propose to go).

I would rather go back a minute and consider whether there was not some good reason behind our initial favouritism for verbs in the so-called 'present indicative active'.

We said that the idea of a performative utterance was that it was to be (or to be included as a part of) the performance of an action. Actions can only be performed by persons, and obviously in our cases the utterer must be the performer: hence our justifiable feeling—which we wrongly cast into purely grammatical mould—in favour of the 'first person', who must come in, being mentioned or referred to; moreover, if in uttering one is acting, one must be doing something—hence our perhaps ill-expressed favouring of the grammatical present and grammatical active of the verb. There is something which is *at the moment of uttering being done by the person uttering*.

Where there is *not*, in the verbal formula of the utterance, a reference to the person doing the uttering, and so the acting, by means of the pronoun 'I' (or by his personal name), then in fact he will be 'referred to' in one of two ways:

(*a*) In verbal utterances, *by his being the person who does* the uttering—what we may call the utterance-*origin* which is used generally in any system of verbal reference-co-ordinates.

(*b*) In written utterances (or 'inscriptions), *by his appending his signature* (this has to be done because, of course, written utterances are not tethered to their origin in the way spoken ones are).

The 'I' who is doing the action does thus come essentially into the picture. An advantage of the original first person singular present indicative active form—or likewise of the second and third and impersonal passive forms with signature appended—is that this implicit feature of the speech-situation is made *explicit*. Moreover, the verbs which seem, on grounds of vocabulary, to be specially performative verbs serve the special purpose of *making explicit* (which is not the same as stating or describing) what precise action it is that is being performed by the issuing of the utterance: other words which seem to have a special performative function (and indeed *have* it), such as 'guilty', 'off-side', &c., do so because, in so far as and when they are linked in 'origin' with these special explicit performative verbs like 'promise', pronounce', 'find', &c.

The 'hereby' formula is a useful alternative; but it is rather too formal for ordinary purposes, and further, we may say 'I hereby state . . .' or 'I hereby question . . .', whereas we were hoping to find a criterion to distinguish statements from performatives. (I must explain again that we are floundering here. To feel the firm ground of prejudice slipping away is exhilarating, but brings its revenges.)

Thus what we should feel tempted to say is that any utterance which is in fact a performative should be reducible, or expandible, or analysable into a form, or reproducible in a form, with a verb in the first person singular present indicative active (grammatical). This is the sort of test we were in fact using above. Thus:

'Out' is equivalent to 'I declare, pronounce, give, or call you out' (when it is a performative: it need not be, for example, if you are called out by someone not the umpire or recorded as 'out' by the scorer).

'Guilty' is equivalent to 'I find, pronounce, deem you to be guilty.'

'You are warned that the bull is dangerous' is equivalent to 'I, John Jones, warn you that the bull is dangerous' or

> This bull is dangerous.
> (Signed) John Jones.

This sort of expansion makes explicit both that the utterance is performative, and which act it is that is being performed. Unless the performative utterance is reduced to such an explicit form, it will regularly be possible to take it in a non-performative way: for example, 'it is yours' may be taken as equivalent to either 'I give it you' or 'it (already) belongs to you'. In fact there is rather a play on the performative and non-performative uses in the road sign 'You have been warned'.

However, though we might make progress along these lines (there are snags)[1] we must notice that this first

[1] For example, which are the verbs with which we can do this? If the performative is expanded, what is the test whether the first person singular present indicative active is on this occasion performative granted that all others have to be reducible (save the mark!) to this normal form?

person singular present indicative active, so called, is a *peculiar and special use*. In particular we must notice that there is an *asymmetry* of a systematic kind between it and other persons and tenses of the *very same verb*. The fact that there is *this* asymmetry is precisely the mark of the performative verb (and the nearest thing to a *grammatical* criterion in connexion with performatives).

Let us take an example: the uses of 'I bet' as opposed to the use of that verb in another tense or in another person. 'I betted' and 'he bets' are not performatives but describe actions on my and his part respectively—actions each consisting in the utterance of the performative 'I bet'. If I utter the words 'I bet . . .', I do not state that I utter the words 'I bet', or any other words, but I perform the act of betting; and similarly, if he says he bets, i.e. says the words 'I bet', he *bets*. But if I utter the words 'he bets', I only state that he utters (or rather has uttered) the words 'I bet': I do not perform his act of betting, which only he can perform: I describe his performances of the act of betting, but I do my own betting, and he must do his own. Similarly an anxious parent when his child has been asked to do something may say 'he promises, don't you Willy?' but little Willy must still himself say 'I promise' if he is really to have promised. Now this sort of asymmetry does not arise at all in general with verbs that are not used as explicit performatives. For example, there is no such asymmetry between 'I run' and 'He runs'.

Still, it is doubtful whether this is a 'grammatical'

criterion exactly (what is?), and anyway it is not very exact because:

(1) The first person singular present indicative active may be used to describe how I habitually behave: 'I bet him (every morning) sixpence that it will rain' or 'I promise only when I intend to keep my word'.

(2) The first person singular present indicative active may be used in a way similar to the 'historic' present. It may be used to describe my own performances elsewhere and elsewhen: 'on page 49 I protest against the verdict'. We might back this up by saying that performative verbs are not used in the present continuous tense (in the first person singular active): we do not say 'I am promising', and 'I am protesting'. But even this is not entirely true, because I can say 'Don't bother me at the moment; I will see you later; I am marrying' at any moment during the ceremony when I am not having to say other words such as 'I do'; here the utterance of the performative is not the whole of the performance, which is protracted and contains diverse elements. Or I can say 'I am protesting' when performing the act by, in this case, means other than saying 'I protest', for example by chaining myself to park railings. Or I can even say 'I am ordering' while writing the words 'I order'.

(3) Some verbs may be used in the first person singular present indicative active simultaneously in two ways. An example is 'I call', as when I say 'I call inflation too much money chasing too few goods' which embraces both a

performative utterance and a description of a naturally consequent performance.

(4) We shall be in apparent danger of bringing in many formulas which we might not like to class as performatives; for example 'I state that' (to utter which *is* to state) as well as 'I bet that'. In both examples there is the same asymmetry between first person and other uses.

(5) We have cases of suiting the action to the word: thus I may say 'I spit me of you' or *j'adoube* said when I give check, or 'I quote' followed by actually quoting. If I define by saying 'I define *x* as follows: *x* is *y*', this is a case of suiting the action (here giving a definition) to the word; when we use the formula 'I define *x* as *y*' we have a transition to a performative utterance from suiting the action to the word. We might add, too, that there is likewise a transition from the use of words as what we may call markers, to performatives. There is a transition from the word END at the end of a novel to the expression 'message ends' at the end of a signal message, to the expression 'with that I conclude my case' as said by Counsel in a law court. These, we may say, are cases of *marking* the action by the word, where eventually the use of the word comes to be the action of 'ending' (a difficult act to perform, being the cessation of acting, or to make explicit in other ways, of course).

(6) Is it always the case that we must have a performative verb for making explicit something we are undoubtedly doing by saying something? For example, I

may insult you by saying something, but we have not the formula 'I insult you'.

(7) Is it really the case that we can always put a performative into the normal form without loss? 'I shall . . .' can be meant in different ways; perhaps we trade on this. Or again we say 'I am sorry'; is this really exactly like the explicit 'I apologize'?

We shall have to revert to the notion of the explicit performative, and we must discuss *historically* at least how some of these perhaps not ultimately serious perplexities arise.

LECTURE VI

BECAUSE we suggested that the performative is not altogether so obviously distinct from the constative—the former happy or unhappy, the latter true or false—we were considering how to define the performative more clearly. The first suggestion was a criterion or criteria of grammar or of vocabulary or of both. We pointed out that there was certainly no one absolute criterion of this kind: and that very probably it is not possible to lay down even a list of all possible criteria; moreover, they certainly would not distinguish performatives from constatives, as very commonly the *same* sentence is used on different occasions of utterance in *both* ways, performative and constative. The thing seems hopeless from the start, if we are to leave utterances *as they stand* and seek for a criterion.

But nevertheless the type of performative upon which we drew for our first examples, which has a verb in the first person singular present indicative active, seems to deserve our favour: at least, if issuing the utterance is doing something, the 'I' and the 'active' and the 'present' seem appropriate. Though indeed performatives are not really like the remainder of the verbs in this 'tense' at all; there is an essential *asymmetry* with these verbs. This asymmetry is just the characteristic of a long list of performative-looking verbs. The suggestion is, then, that we might

   (1) make a list of all verbs with this peculiarity;
   (2) suppose that all performative utterances which are not in fact in this preferred form—beginning 'I *x* that', 'I *x* to', or 'I *x*'—could be 'reduced' to this form and so rendered what we may call *explicit* performatives.

We are now asking: just how easy—even possible—is this going to be? It is fairly easy to make allowances for certain normal enough but different uses of the first person of the present indicative active even with these verbs, which may well be constative or descriptive, that is, the habitual present, the 'historic' (quasi-) present, and the continuous present. But then, as I was hastily mentioning, in conclusion, there are still further difficulties: we mentioned three as typical.

   (1) 'I class' or perhaps 'I hold' seems in a way one, in a way the other. Which is it, or is it both?

   (2) 'I state that' seems to conform to our grammatical or quasi-grammatical requirements: but do we want *it* in? Our criterion, such as it is, seems in danger of letting in non-performatives.

   (3) Sometimes saying something seems to be characteristically doing something—for example insulting somebody, like reprimanding somebody: yet there is no performative 'I insult you'. Our criterion will not get in all cases of the issuing of an utterance being the

doing of something, because the 'reduction' to an explicit performative does not seem always possible.

Let us pause then to dwell a little more on the expression 'explicit performative', which we have introduced rather surreptitiously. I shall oppose it to 'primary performative' (rather than to inexplicit or implicit performative). We gave as an example:

(1) primary utterance: 'I shall be there',

(2) explicit performative: 'I promise that I shall be there', and we said that the latter formula made explicit what action it is that is being performed in issuing the utterance: i.e. 'I shall be there'. If someone says 'I shall be there', we might ask: 'Is that a promise?' We may receive the answer 'Yes', or 'Yes, I promise it' (or 'that ...' or 'to...'), whereas the answer might have been only: 'No, but I do intend to be' (expressing or announcing an intention), or 'No, but I can foresee that, knowing my weaknesses, I (probably) shall be there'.

Now we must enter two caveats: 'making explicit' is not the same as describing or stating (at least in philosophers' preferred senses of these words) what I am doing. If 'making explicit' conveys this, then *pro tanto* it is a bad term. The situation in the case of actions which are non-linguistic but similar to performative utterances in that they are the performance of a conventional action (here ritual or ceremonial) is rather like this: suppose I bow deeply before you; it might not be clear whether I am doing obeisance to you or, say, stooping to observe the flora or to ease my indigestion. Generally speaking,

then, to make clear both *that* it is a conventional ceremonial act, and *which* act it is, the act (for example of
doing obeisance) will as a rule include some special
further feature, for example raising my hat, tapping my
head on the ground, sweeping my other hand to my
heart, or even very likely uttering some noise or word, for
example 'Salaam'. Now uttering 'Salaam' is no more
describing my performance, stating that I am performing
an act of obeisance, than is taking off my hat: and by the
same token (though we shall come back to this) saying
'I salute you' is no more describing my performance
than is saying 'Salaam'. To do or to say these things is to
make plain how the action is to be taken or understood,
what action it is. And so it is with putting in the expression
'I promise that'. It is not a description, because (1) it
could not be false, nor, therefore, true; (2) saying 'I
promise that' (if happy, of course) *makes it* a promise, and
makes it unambiguously a promise. Now we can say that
such a performative formula as 'I promise' makes it
clear how what is said is to be understood and even
conceivably that the formula 'states that' a promise has
been made; but we cannot say that such utterances are
true or false, nor that they are descriptions or reports.

Secondly, a minor caution: notice that, although we
have in this type of utterance a 'that-' clause following a
verb, for example 'promise', or 'find', or 'pronounce' (or
perhaps such verbs as 'estimate'), we must not allude to
this as 'indirect speech'. 'That'-clauses in indirect speech
or *oratio obliqua* are of course cases where I report what

someone else or myself elsewhen or elsewhere did say: for example, typically, 'he said that . . .', but also possibly 'he promised that . . .' (or is this a double use of 'that'?), or 'on page 456 I declared that . . .'. If this is a clear notion[1] we see that the 'that' of *oratio obliqua* is not in all ways similar to the 'that' in our explicit performative formulas: here I am not reporting my own speech in the first person singular present indicative active. Incidentally, of course, it is not in the least necessary that an explicit performative verb should be followed by 'that': in important classes of cases it is followed by 'to . . .' or nothing, for example, 'I apologize (for . . .)', 'I salute you'.

Now, one thing that seems at least a fair guess, even from the elaboration of the linguistic construction, as also from its nature in the explicit performative is this: that historically, from the point of view of the evolution of language, the explicit performative must be a later development than certain more primary utterances, many of which at least are already implicit performatives, which are included in most or many explicit performatives as parts of a whole. For example, 'I will . . .' is earlier than 'I promise that I will . . .'. The plausible view (I do not know exactly how it would be established) would be that in primitive languages it would not yet be clear, it would not yet be possible to distinguish, which of various things that (using later distinctions) we might be doing

[1] My explanation is very obscure, like those of all grammar books on 'that' clauses: compare their even worse explanation of 'what' clauses.

we were in fact doing. For example 'Bull' or 'Thunder' in a primitive language of one-word utterances[1] could be a warning, information, a prediction, &c. It is also a plausible view that explicitly distinguishing the different *forces* that this utterance might have is a later achievement of language, and a considerable one; primitive or primary forms of utterance will preserve the 'ambiguity' or 'equivocation' or 'vagueness' of primitive language in this respect; they will not make explicit the precise force of the utterance. This may have its uses: but sophistication and development of social forms and procedures will necessitate clarification. But note that this clarification is as much a creative act as a discovery or description! It is as much a matter of making clear distinctions as of making already existent distinctions clear.

One thing, however, that it will be most dangerous to do, and that we are very prone to do, is to take it that we somehow *know* that the primary or primitive use of sentences must be, because it ought to be, statemental or constative, in the philosophers' preferred sense of simply uttering something whose sole pretension is to be true or false and which is not liable to criticism in any other dimension. We certainly do not know that this is so, any more, for example, than that all utterances must have first begun as imperatives (as some argue) or as swear-words—and it seems much more likely that the 'pure' statement is a goal, an ideal, towards which the gradual development of science has given the impetus, as it has

[1] As in fact primitive languages probably were, cf. Jespersen.

likewise also towards the goal of precision. Language as such and in its primitive stages is not precise, and it is also not, in our sense, explicit: precision in language makes it clearer what is being said—its *meaning*: explicitness, in our sense, makes clearer the *force* of the utterances, or 'how (in one sense; see below) it is to be taken'.

The explicit performative formula, moreover, is only the last and 'most successful' of numerous speech-devices which have always been used with greater or less success to perform the same function (just as measurement or standardization was the most successful device ever invented for developing *precision* of speech).

Consider for a moment *some* of these other more primitive devices in speech, some of the roles which can (though, of course, not without change or loss, as we shall see) be taken over by the device of the explicit performative.

1. *Mood*

We have already mentioned the exceedingly common device of using the imperative mood. This makes the utterance a 'command' (or an exhortation or permission or concession or what not!) Thus I may say 'shut it' in many contexts:

'Shut it, do' resembles 'I order you to shut it'.

'Shut it—I should' resembles 'I advise you to shut it'.

'Shut it, if you like' resembles 'I permit you to shut it'.

'Very well then, shut it' resembles 'I consent to your shutting it'.

'Shut it if you dare' resembles 'I dare you to shut it'.

Or again we may use auxiliaries:

'You may shut it' resembles 'I give permission, I consent, to your shutting it'.

'You must shut it' resembles 'I order you, I advise you, to shut it'.

'You ought to shut it' resembles 'I advise you to shut it'.

2. *Tone of voice, cadence, emphasis*

(Similar to this is the sophisticated device of using stage directions; for example, 'threateningly', &c.) Examples of this are:

> It's going to charge! (a warning);
> It's going to charge? (a question);
> It's going to charge!? (a protest).

These features of spoken language are not reproducible readily in written language. For example we have tried to convey the tone of voice, cadence and emphasis of a protest by the use of an exclamation mark and a question mark (but this is very jejune). Punctuation, italics, and word order may help, but they are rather crude.

3. *Adverbs and adverbial phrases*

But in written language—and even, to some extent, in spoken language, though there they are not so necessary —we rely on adverbs, adverbial phrases, or turns of phrase. Thus we can qualify the force of 'I shall' by adding 'probably' or—in an opposite sense—by adding 'without fail'; we can give emphasis (to a reminder or whatever it may be) by writing 'You would do well never to forget that . . .'. Much could be said about the connexions here with the phenomena of evincing, intimating, insinuation, innuendo, giving to understand, enabling to infer, conveying, 'expressing' (odious word) all of which are, however, essentially different, though they involve the employment of very often the same or similar verbal devices and circumlocutions. In the latter half of our lectures we shall revert to the important and difficult distinction which needs to be drawn here.

4. *Connecting particles*

At a more sophisticated level, perhaps, comes the use of the special verbal device of the connecting particle; thus we may use the particle 'still' with the force of 'I insist that'; we use 'therefore' with the force of 'I conclude that'; we use 'although' with the force of 'I concede that'. Note also the uses of 'whereas' and 'hereby' and 'moreover'.[1] A very similar purpose is served by the use of titles such as Manifesto, Act, Proclamation, or the subheading 'A Novel . . .'.

Moreover, even apart from and turning from what we say and the manner of speaking it, there are other

---

[1] But some of these examples raise the old question whether 'I concede that' and 'I conclude that' are performatives or not.

essential devices by which the force of the utterance is to some extent got across:

5. *Accompaniments of the utterance*

We may accompany the utterance of the words by gestures (winks, pointings, shruggings, frowns, &c.) or by ceremonial non-verbal actions. These may sometimes serve without the utterance of any words, and their importance is very obvious.

6. *The circumstances of the utterance*

An exceedingly important aid is the circumstances of the utterance. Thus we may say 'coming from *him*, I took it as an order, not as a request'; similarly the context of the words 'I shall die some day', 'I shall leave you my watch', in particular the health of the speaker, make a difference how we shall understand them.

But in a way these resources are over-rich: they lend themselves to equivocation and inadequate discrimination; and moreover, we use them for other purposes, e.g. insinuation. The explicit performative rules out equivocation and keeps the performance fixed, relatively.

The trouble about all these devices has been principally their vagueness of meaning and uncertainty of sure reception, but there is also probably some positive inadequacy in them for dealing with anything like the complexity of the field of actions which we perform with words. An 'imperative' may be an order, a permission, a demand, a request, an entreaty, a suggestion, a recommendation, a warning ('go and you will see'), or may express a condition or concession or a definition ('Let it . . .'), &c. To hand something over to someone may be, when we say 'Take it', the giving it or lending it or leasing it or entrusting it. To say 'I shall' may be to promise, or to express an intention, or to forecast my future. And so on. No doubt a combination of some or all the devices mentioned above (and very likely there are others) will usually, if not in the end, suffice. Thus when we say 'I shall' we can make it clear that we are forecasting by adding the adverbs 'undoubtedly' or 'probably', that we are expressing an intention by adding the adverbs 'certainly' or 'definitely', or that we are promising by adding the adverbial phrase 'without fail', or saying 'I shall do my best to'.

It should be noted that when performative verbs exist we can use them not only in 'that . . .' or 'to . . .' formulas, but also in stage directions ('welcomes'), titles ('warning!'), and parentheses (this is almost as good a test of a performative as our normal forms); and we must not forget the use of special words such as 'Out', &c., which have no normal form.

However, the existence and even the use of explicit performatives does not remove all our troubles.

(1) In philosophy, we can even raise the trouble of the liability of performatives to be mistaken for descriptives or constatives.

(1a) Nor, of course, is it merely that the performative does not preserve the often congenial equivocation of primary utterances; we must also in passing consider cases where it is doubtful whether the expression is an explicit performative or not and cases very similar to performatives but not performatives.

(2) There seem to be clear cases where the very same formula seems sometimes to be an explicit performative and sometimes to be a descriptive, and may even trade on this ambivalence: for example, 'I approve' and 'I agree'. Thus 'I approve' may have the performative force of giving approval or it may have a descriptive meaning: 'I favour this'.

We shall consider two classic sorts of case in which this will arise. They exhibit some of the phenomena incidental to the development of explicit performative formulas.

There are numerous cases in human life where the feeling of a certain 'emotion' (save the word!) or 'wish' or the adoption of an attitude is conventionally considered an appropriate or fitting response or reaction to a certain state of affairs, including the performance by someone of a certain act, cases where such a response is natural (or we should like to think so!) In such cases it is, of course, possible and usual actually to feel the emotion or wish in question; and since our emotions or wishes are not readily detectable by others, it is common to wish to inform others that we have them. Understandably, though for slightly different and perhaps less estimable reasons in different cases, it becomes *de rigueur* to 'express' these feelings if we have them, and further even to express them when they are felt fitting, regardless of whether we really feel anything at all which we are reporting. Examples of expressions so used are:

I thank	I am grateful	I feel grateful
I apologize	I am sorry	I repent
I criticize⎫ I censure⎭	I blame	⎧ I am shocked by ⎩ I am revolted by
I approve	I approve of	I feel approval
I bid you welcome	I welcome	
I congratulate	I am glad about	

In these lists, the first column contains performative utterances; those in the second are not pure but half descriptive, and in the third are merely reports. There are then here numerous expressions, among them many important ones, which suffer from or profit by a sort of deliberate ambivalence, and this is fought by the constant introduction of deliberately pure performative phrases. Can we suggest any tests for deciding whether 'I approve of' or 'I am sorry' is being used (or even is always used) in the one way or the other?

One test would be whether it makes sense to say 'Does he *really*?' For example, when someone says 'I welcome you' or 'I bid you welcome', we may say 'I wonder if he really did welcome him?' though we could not say in the same way 'I wonder whether he really does bid him welcome?' Another test would be whether one could really be doing it without actually saying anything, for example in the case of being sorry as distinct from apologizing, in being grateful as distinct from thanking, in blaming as distinct from censuring.[1] Yet a third test would be, at least in some cases, to ask whether we could insert before the supposed performative verb some such adverb as 'deliberately' or such an expression as 'I am willing to': because (possibly) if the utterance is the doing of an action, then it is surely something we ought to be able (on occasion) to do deliberately or to be willing to do. Thus we may say: 'I deliberately bade him welcome', 'I deliberately approved his action', 'I deliberately apologized', and we can say 'I am willing to apologize'. But we cannot say 'I deliberately approved of his action' or 'I am willing to be sorry' (as distinct from 'I am willing to say I am sorry').

A fourth test would be to ask whether what one says could be literally false, as sometimes when I say 'I am sorry', or could only involve insincerity (unhappiness) as sometimes when I say 'I apologize': these phrases blur the distinction between insincerity and falsehood.[2]

But there is here a certain distinction to be drawn in passing of the exact nature of which I am uncertain: we have related 'I apologize' to 'I am sorry' as above; but now there are also very numerous conventional expressions of feeling, very similar in some ways, which are

---

[1] There are classic doubts about the possibility of tacit consent; here non-verbal performance occurs in an alternative form of performative act: this casts doubt on this second test!

[2] There are parallel phenomena to these in other cases: for example a specially confusing one arises over what we may call dictional or expositive performatives.

certainly nothing to do with performatives: for example:

'I have pleasure in calling upon the next speaker'.

'I am sorry to have to say . . .'.

'I am gratified to be in a position to announce . . .'.[1]

We may call these *polite* phrases, like 'I have the honour to . . .'. It is conventional enough to formulate them in this way: but it is *not* the case that to say you have pleasure in *is* to have pleasure in doing something. Unfortunately. To be a performative utterance, even in these cases connected with feelings and attitudes which I christen 'BEHABITIVES', is not *merely* to be a conventional expression of feeling or attitude.

Also to be distinguished are cases of *suiting the action to the word*—a special type of case which may generate performatives but which is not in itself a case of the performative utterance. A typical case is: 'I slam the door thus' (he slams the door). But this sort of case leads to 'I salute you' (he salutes); here 'I salute you' may become a substitute for the salute and thus a pure performative utterance. To say 'I salute you' now *is* to salute you. Compare the expression 'I salute the memory . . .'.

But there are many transitional stages between suiting the action to the word and the pure performative:

'Snap.' To say this is to snap (in appropriate circumstances); but it is not a snap if 'snap' is not said.

[1] [Marginal note in manuscript: 'Further classification needed here: just note it in passing.']

'Check.' To say it is to check in appropriate circumstances. But would it not still be a check if 'check' were not said?

'J'adoube.' Is this suiting the action to the word or is it part of the act of straightening the piece as opposed to moving it?

Perhaps these distinctions are not important: but there are similar transitions in the case of performatives, as for example:

'I quote': he quotes.

'I define': he defines (e.g. x is y).

'I define x as y'.

In these cases the utterance operates like a title: is it a variety of performative? It essentially operates where the action suited to the word is itself a verbal performance.

LECTURE VII

LAST time we considered the Explicit in contrast with the Primary Performative, claiming that the former would be naturally evolved from the latter as language and society develop. We said, however, that this would not remove all our troubles in our search for a list of explicit performative verbs. We gave some examples which incidentally illustrated how the explicit performative develops from the primary.

We took examples from the sphere of what may be called *behabitives*, a kind of performative concerned roughly with reactions to behaviour and with behaviour towards others and designed to exhibit attitudes and feelings.

Contrast:

Explicit Performative	*Not Pure (half descriptive)*	*Descriptive*
I apologize	I am sorry	I repent
I criticize⎫ I censure⎭	I blame	I am disgusted by
I approve	I approve of	I feel approval of
I bid you welcome	I welcome you	

We suggested tests of the pure explicit performative:

(1) Does it make sense (or the same sense) to ask 'But

did he *really?*'? We cannot ask 'Did he really bid him welcome?' in the same sense as we ask 'Did he really welcome him?' or 'Did he really criticize him?' in the same sense as we ask 'Did he really blame him?' This is not a very good test because, for example, of the possibility of infelicities. We may ask 'Did he really marry?' when he said 'I do', because there may have been infelicities which made the marriage problematical.

(2) Could he be doing the action without uttering the performative?

(3) Could he do it deliberately?; could he be willing to do it?

(4) Could it be literally false that, for example, I criticize (as distinct from blame) when I have said that I criticize? (It could, of course, be *insincere* always.)

Sometimes the test of a different word, sometimes of a different construction of the formula, is available. Thus in an explicit performative we say 'I approve' rather than 'I approve of'. Compare the distinction between 'I wish you were at the bottom of the sea' and 'I wish you at the bottom of the sea', or between 'I wish you were enjoying yourself' and 'I wish you joy', &c.

In conclusion, we distinguished our performatives from:

(1) Purely polite conventional ritual phrases such as 'I have pleasure in . . .'. These are quite different, in that, although ritual and not called upon to be sincere, they are according to all the four tests above not performatives. They seem to be a limited class, limited perhaps to

professions of feeling and even to professions of feeling at saying or hearing something.

(2) Suiting the action to the word, of which a typical example would be Counsel, at the end of his case saying 'I end my case'. These phrases are especially liable to pass over into pure performatives where the action which is suited to the word is itself a purely ritual action, the non-verbal action of bowing ('I salute you') or the verbal ritual of saying 'Huzza' ('I applaud').

A second very important class of words in which the same phenomenon of a shift from descriptive to performative utterance and wavering between them is, as with behabitives, peculiarly rampant, is the class of what I call *expositives*, or expositional performatives. Here the main body of the utterance has generally or often the straightforward form of a 'statement', but there is an explicit performative verb at its head which shows how the 'statement' is to be fitted into the context of conversation, interlocution, dialogue, or in general of exposition. Here are some examples:

'I argue (or urge) that there is no backside to the moon.'

'I conclude (or infer) that there is no backside to the moon.'

'I testify that there is no backside to the moon.'

'I admit (or concede) that there is no backside to the moon.'

'I prophesy (or predict) that there is no backside to the moon.'

To say such things as these is to argue, conclude, testify, reply, predict, &c.

Now many of these verbs appear to be quite satisfactory pure performatives. (Irritating though it is to have them as such, linked with clauses that look like 'statements', true or false, we have mentioned this before and will return to it again.) For example, when I say 'I prophesy that . . .', 'I concede that . . .', 'I postulate that . . .', the clause following will normally look just like a statement, but the verbs themselves seem to be pure performatives.

To take our four tests that we have used with the behabitives: when he says 'I postulate that . . .' then

(1) we cannot ask 'But was he *really* postulating . . .?'
(2) he cannot be postulating without saying so;
(3) one can say 'I deliberately postulated . . .' or 'I am willing to postulate . . .';

(4) it cannot be literally false to say 'I postulate' (except in the sense already noted: 'on page 265 I postulate . . .'). In all these respects 'I postulate' is like 'I apologize for . . .', 'I criticize him for . . .'. Of course, these utterances can be unhappy—he can predict when he has no right to predict, or say 'I confess you did it', or be insincere by saying 'I confess I did' when he did not.

Yet there are numerous verbs which look very similar, and seem to fall into the same class, which would *not* so satisfactorily pass these tests: as, for example, 'I assume that' as distinct from 'I postulate that'. I should cheerfully say 'I was assuming that . . .' when I did not realize that I was assuming it and without having said anything to that effect. And I may be assuming something, though I don't realize it or say so, in the important descriptive sense. I may, of course, be asserting or denying something, for instance, without saying anything to that effect, where 'I assert' and 'I deny' are pure explicit performatives in some senses which are not here relevant; I may nod or shake my head, or assert or deny it *by implication* in saying something else. But with 'I was assuming that' I could have been assuming something without saying anything, *not* by implication by saying something else, but just by quietly sitting in my corner in a way in which I could not be just quietly sitting in my corner denying it.

In other words 'I assume that...' and perhaps 'I suppose that . . .' operate in the ambivalent way that 'I am sorry for . . .' operates: this sometimes is equivalent to 'I apologize', sometimes describes my feelings, sometimes does both at once; so 'I assume' sometimes is equivalent to 'I postulate . . .' and sometimes is not.

Or again 'I agree that . . .' sometimes operates like 'I approve his conduct', sometimes more like 'I approve of his conduct', where at least in part it describes my attitude, frame of mind, state of belief. Here again slight changes of phrase may be important, for example the difference between 'I agree to . . .' and 'I agree with . . .': but this is not a cast-iron test.

The same general phenomenon occurs with this class

as with behabitives. Just as we have 'I premise that (I postulate that)' as a pure explicit performative where 'I assume that' is not, so we have:

> 'I forecast (predict) that' as a pure explicit performative where 'I foresee (expect, anticipate) that' is not;
> 'I endorse (I assent to) that opinion' as a pure explicit performative where 'I agree with that opinion' is not;
> 'I question whether it is so' as a pure explicit performative where 'I wonder (doubt) whether it is so' is not.

Here 'postulate', 'predict', 'endorse', 'question', &c. will pass all our tests of the pure explicit performative, whereas the others will not, or will not always.

Now one point in passing: not all the things we do in this sort of line in fitting our particular utterance, say, into its context of discourse can be things that we can do by an explicit performative. For example, we cannot say 'I imply that', 'I insinuate', &c.

Behabitives and expositives are two very critical classes in which this phenomenon occurs: but it is also found in other classes, for example in what I call *verdictives*. Examples of verdictives are 'I pronounce that . . .', 'I hold that . . .', 'I make it . . .', 'I date it . . .'. Thus if you are a judge and say 'I hold that . . .' then to say you hold is to hold; with less official persons it is not so clearly so: it may be merely descriptive of a state of mind. This difficulty may be avoided in the usual manner by the invention of a special word such as 'verdict', 'I find *in* favour of . . .', 'I pronounce . . .'; otherwise the performative nature of the utterance still depends partly on the context of the utterance, such as the judge being a judge and in robes on a bench, &c.

Somewhat similar to this would be the case of 'I class *x*'s as *y*'s', where we saw there was a double use: the pure explicit performative which commits me to certain future conduct, and then the description, not of my state of mind, but of my regular behaviour. We may say 'He does not really class . . .' or 'He is classing . . .' and he may be classing without saying anything. We must distinguish this use from those in which we are committed to certain regular acts by the performance of the single act: for example 'I define *x* as *y*' does not state that he regularly does so but commits him to certain regular acts of using one expression as equivalent to another. In this context it is instructive to compare 'I intend' with 'I promise'.

So much for this sort of problem, whether an apparent or suggested explicit performative verb itself operates, or operates sometimes or in part, as a description, true or false, of feelings, states of mind, frames of mind, &c. But this type of case suggests again the wider phenomenon to which attention has been drawn, where the whole utterance seems essentially meant to be true or false despite its performative characteristics. Even if we take such half-way houses as, say, 'I hold that . . .' as said by a non-juryman, or 'I expect that. . .', it seems absurd to suppose that all they describe or state, so far as they do this or when they do, is something about the speaker's beliefs or expectations. To suppose this is rather the sort of Alice-in-Wonderland over-sharpness of taking 'I think that p' as a statement about yourself which could be answered: 'That is just a fact about you'. ('I don't think . . .' began Alice: 'then you should not talk' said the Caterpillar or whoever it was). And when we come to pure explicit performatives such as 'state' or 'maintain', surely the whole thing is true or false even though the uttering of it is the performing of the action of stating or maintaining. And we have repeatedly pointed out that some things that are quite clearly classic performatives like 'Over' bear a very close relation to describing facts, even if others like 'Play' do not.

This, however, is not so bad: we could distinguish the performative opening part (I state that) which makes clear how the utterance is to be taken, that it is a statement (as distinct from a prediction, &c.), from the bit in the that-clause which is required to be true or false. However, there are many cases which, as language stands at present, we are not able to split into two parts in this way, even though the utterance seems to have a sort of explicit performative in it: thus 'I liken x to y', 'I analyse x as y'. Here we both do the likening and assert that there is a likeness by means of one compendious phrase of at least a quasi-performative character. Just to spur us on our way: we may also mention 'I know that', 'I believe that', &c. How complicated are these examples? We cannot assume that they are purely descriptive.

Now let us consider where we stand for a moment: beginning with the supposed contrast between performative and constative utterances, we found sufficient indications that unhappiness nevertheless seems to characterize both kinds of utterance, not merely the performative; and that the requirement of conforming or bearing some relation to the facts, different in different cases, seems to characterize performatives, in addition to the requirement that they should be happy, similarly to the way which is characteristic of supposed constatives.

Now we failed to find a grammatical criterion for performatives, but we thought that perhaps we could insist that every performative *could* be in principle put into the form of an explicit performative, and then we could make a list of performative verbs. Since then we have found, however, that it is often not easy to be sure that, even when it is apparently in explicit form, an utterance is performative or that it is not; and typically anyway, we still have utterances beginning 'I state that . . .' which seem to satisfy the requirements of being performative, yet which surely are the making of statements, and surely are essentially true or false.

It is time then to make a fresh start on the problem. We want to reconsider more generally the senses in which to say something may be to do something, or in saying something we do something (and also perhaps to consider the different case in which *by* saying something we do something). Perhaps some clarification and definition here may help us out of our tangle. For after all, 'doing something' is a very vague expression. When we issue any utterance[1] whatsoever, are we not 'doing something'? Certainly the ways in which we talk about 'action' are liable here, as elsewhere, to be confusing. For example, we may contrast men of words with men of action, we may say they *did* nothing, only talked or *said* things: yet again, we may contrast *only* thinking something with *actually* saying it (out loud), in which context saying it *is* doing something.

It is time to refine upon the circumstances of 'issuing an utterance'.[2] To begin with, there is a whole group of senses, which I shall label (A), in which to say anything must always be to do something, the group of senses which together add up to 'saying' something, in the full sense of 'say'. We may agree, without insisting on formulations or refinements, that to say anything is

(A. *a*) always to perform the act of uttering certain noises (a 'phonetic' act), and the utterance is a phone;

(A. *b*) always to perform the act of uttering certain vocables or words, i.e. noises of certain types belonging to *and as* belonging to a certain vocabulary, in a certain construction, i.e. conforming to and as conforming to a certain grammar, with a certain intonation, &c. This act we may call a 'phatic' act, and the utterance which it is the act of uttering a 'pheme' (as

---

[1] I use 'utterance' only as equivalent to *utteratum*: for *utteratio* I use 'the issuing of an utterance'.

[2] We shall not always mention but must bear in mind the possibility of 'etiolation' as it occurs when we use speech in acting, fiction and poetry, quotation and recitation.

distinct from the phememe of linguistic theory);
and

(A. *c*) generally to perform the act of using that pheme or
its constituents with a certain more or less definite
'sense' and a more or less definite 'reference' (which
together are equivalent to 'meaning'). This act we may
call a 'rhetic' act, and the utterance which it is the act
of uttering a 'rheme'.

LECTURE VIII

IN embarking on a programme of finding a list of explicit performative verbs, it seemed that we were going to find it not always easy to distinguish performative utterances from constative, and it therefore seemed expedient to go farther back for a while to fundamentals—to consider from the ground up how many senses there are in which to say something *is* to do something, or *in* saying something we do something, and even *by* saying something we do something. And we began by distinguishing a whole group of senses of 'doing something' which are all included together when we say, what is obvious, that to say something is in the full normal sense to do something—which includes the utterance of certain noises, the utterance of certain words in a certain construction, and the utterance of them with a certain 'meaning' in the favourite philosophical sense of that word, i.e. with a certain sense and with a certain reference.

The act of 'saying something' in this full normal sense I call, i.e. dub, the performance of a locutionary act, and the study of utterances thus far and in these respects the study of locutions, or of the full units of speech. Our interest in the locutionary act is, of course, principally to make quite plain what it is, in order to distinguish it from other acts with which we are going to be primarily concerned. Let me add merely that, of course, a great many further refinements would be possible and necessary if we were to discuss it for its own sake—refinements of very great importance not merely to philosophers but to, say, grammarians and phoneticians.

We had made three rough distinctions between the phonetic act, the phatic act, and the rhetic act. The phonetic act is merely the act of uttering certain noises. The phatic act is the uttering of certain vocables or words, i.e. noises of certain types, belonging to and as belonging to, a certain vocabulary, conforming to and as conforming to a certain grammar. The rhetic act is the performance of an act of using those vocables with a certain more-or-less definite sense and reference. Thus 'He said "The cat is on the mat"', reports a phatic act, whereas 'He said that the cat was on the mat' reports a rhetic act. A similar contrast is illustrated by the pairs:

'He said "The cat is on the mat"', 'He said (that) the cat was on the mat';
'He said "I shall be there"', 'He said he would be there';
'He said "Get out"', 'He told me to get out';
'He said "Is it in Oxford or Cambridge?"'; 'He asked whether it was in Oxford or Cambridge'.

To pursue this for its own sake beyond our immediate requirements, I shall mention some general points worth remembering:

(1) Obviously, to perform a phatic I must perform a

phonetic act, or, if you like, in performing one I am performing the other (not, however, that phatic acts are a sub-class of phonetic acts; we defined the phatic act as the uttering of vocables *as* belonging to a certain vocabulary): but the converse is not true, for if a monkey makes a noise indistinguishable from 'go' it is still not a phatic act.

(2) Obviously in the definition of the phatic act two things were lumped together: vocabulary and grammar. So we have not assigned a special name to the person who utters, for example, 'cat thoroughly the if' or 'the slithy toves did gyre'. Yet a further point arising is the intonation as well as grammar and vocabulary.

(3) The phatic act, however, like the phonetic, is essentially mimicable, reproducible (including intonation, winks, gestures, &c.). One can mimic not merely the statement in quotation marks 'She has lovely hair', but also the more complex fact that he said it like this: 'She has lovely *hair*' (shrugs).

This is the 'inverted commas' use of 'said' as we get it in novels: every utterance can be just reproduced in inverted commas, or in inverted commas with 'said he' or, more often, 'said she', &c., after it.

But the rhetic act is the one we report, in the case of assertions, by saying 'He said that the cat was on the mat', 'He said he would go', 'He said I was to go' (his words were 'You are to go'). This is the so-called 'indirect speech'. If the sense or reference is *not* being taken as clear, then the whole or part is to be in quotation marks. Thus

I might say: 'He said I was to go to "the minister", but he did not say which minister' or 'I said that he was behaving badly and he replied that "the higher you get the fewer" '. We cannot, however, always use 'said that' easily: we would say 'told to', 'advise to', &c., if he used the imperative mood, or such equivalent phrases as 'said I was to', 'said I should', &c. Compare such phrases as 'bade me welcome' and 'extended his apologies'.

I add one further point about the rhetic act: of course sense and reference (naming and referring) themselves are here ancillary acts performed in performing the rhetic act. Thus we may say 'I meant by "bank" . . .' and we say 'by "he" I was referring to . . .'. Can we perform a rhetic act without referring or without naming? In general it would seem that the answer is that we cannot, but there are puzzling cases. What is the reference in 'all triangles have three sides'? Correspondingly, it is clear that we can perform a phatic act which is not a rhetic act, though not conversely. Thus we may repeat someone else's remark or mumble over some sentence, or we may read a Latin sentence without knowing the meaning of the words.

The question when one pheme or one rheme is the *same* as another, whether in the 'type' or 'token' sense, and the question what is one single pheme or rheme, do not so much matter here. But, of course, it is important to remember that the same pheme, e.g., sentence, that is, · tokens of the same type, may be used on different occasions of utterance with a different sense or reference, and so be a different rheme. When different phemes are used with the same sense and reference, we might speak of rhetically equivalent acts ('the same statement' in one sense) but not of the same rheme or rhetic acts (which are the same statement in another sense which involves using the same words).

The pheme is a unit of *language*: its typical fault is to be nonsense—meaningless. But the rheme is a unit of *speech*; its typical fault is to be vague or void or obscure, &c.

But though these matters are of much interest, they do not so far throw any light at all on our problem of the constative as opposed to the performative utterance. For example, it might be perfectly possible, with regard to an utterance, say 'It is going to charge', to make entirely plain 'what we were saying' in issuing the utterance, in all the senses so far distinguished, and yet not at all to have cleared up whether or not in issuing the utterance I was performing the act of *warning* or not. It may be perfectly clear what I mean by 'It is going to charge' or 'Shut the door', but not clear whether it is meant as a statement or warning, &c.

To perform a locutionary act is in general, we may say, also and *eo ipso* to perform an *illocutionary* act, as I propose to call it. Thus in performing a locutionary act we shall also be performing such an act as:

asking or answering a question,
giving some information or an assurance or a warning,
announcing a verdict or an intention,

pronouncing sentence,

making an appointment or an appeal or a criticism,

making an identification or giving a description,

and the numerous like. (I am not suggesting that this is a clearly defined class by any means.) There is nothing mysterious about our *eo ipso* here. The trouble rather is the number of different senses of so vague an expression as 'in what way are we using it'—this may refer even to a locutionary act, and further to perlocutionary acts to which we shall come in a minute. When we perform a locutionary act, we use speech: but in what way precisely are we using it on this occasion? For there are very numerous functions of or ways in which we use speech, and it makes a great difference to our act in some sense— sense (B)[1]—in which way and which *sense* we were on this occasion 'using' it. It makes a great difference whether we were advising, or merely suggesting, or actually ordering, whether we were strictly promising or only announcing a vague intention, and so forth. These issues penetrate a little but not without confusion into grammar (see above), but we constantly do debate them, in such terms as whether certain words (a certain locution) *had the force of* a question, or *ought to have been taken as* an estimate and so on.

I explained the performance of an act in this new and second sense as the performance of an 'illocutionary' act, i.e. performance of an act *in* saying something as opposed

---

[1] See below, p. 101.

to performance of an act *of* saying something; I call the act performed an 'illocution' and shall refer to the doctrine of the different types of function of language here in question as the doctrine of 'illocutionary forces'.

It may be said that for too long philosophers have neglected this study, treating all problems as problems of 'locutionary usage', and indeed that the 'descriptive fallacy' mentioned in Lecture I commonly arises through mistaking a problem of the former kind for a problem of the latter kind. True, we are now getting out of this; for some years we have been realizing more and more clearly that the occasion of an utterance matters seriously, and that the words used are to some extent to be 'explained' by the 'context' in which they are designed to be or have actually been spoken in a linguistic interchange. Yet still perhaps we are too prone to give these explanations in terms of 'the meanings of words'. Admittedly we can use 'meaning' also with reference to illocutionary force— 'He meant it as an order', &c. But I want to distinguish *force* and meaning in the sense in which meaning is equivalent to sense and reference, just as it has become essential to distinguish sense and reference.

Moreover, we have here an illustration of the different uses of the expression, 'uses of language', or 'use of a sentence', &c.—'use' is a hopelessly ambiguous or wide word, just as is the word 'meaning', which it has become customary to deride. But 'use', its supplanter, is not in much better case. We may entirely clear up the 'use of a sentence' on a particular occasion, in the sense of the locutionary act, without yet touching upon its use in the sense of an *illocutionary* act.

Before refining any further on this notion of the illocutionary act, let us contrast both the locutionary *and* the illocutionary act with yet a third kind of act.

There is yet a further sense (C) in which to perform a locutionary act, and therein an illocutionary act, may also be to perform an act of another kind. Saying something will often, or even normally, produce certain consequential effects upon the feelings, thoughts, or actions of the audience, or of the speaker, or of other persons: and it may be done with the design, intention, or purpose of producing them; and we may then say, thinking of this, that the speaker has performed an act in the nomenclature of which reference is made either (C. *a*), only obliquely, or even (C. *b*), not at all, to the performance of the locutionary or illocutionary act. We shall call the performance of an act of this kind the performance of a 'perlocutionary' act, and the act performed, where suitable—essentially in cases falling under (C. *a*)—a 'perlocution'. Let us not yet define this idea any more carefully—of course it needs it—but simply give examples:

(E. 1)

Act (A) or Locution

He said to me 'Shoot her!' meaning by 'shoot' shoot and referring by 'her' to *her*.

Act (B)   or Illocution

He urged (or advised, ordered, &c.) me to shoot her.

Act (C. *a*)   or Perlocution

He persuaded me to shoot her.

Act (C. *b*)

He got me to (or made me, &c.) shoot her.

(E. 2)

Act (A)   or Locution

He said to me, 'You can't do that'.

Act (B)   or Illocution

He protested against my doing it.

Act (C. *a*)   or Perlocution

He pulled me up, checked me.

Act (C. *b*)

He stopped me, he brought me to my senses, &c.
He annoyed me.

We can similarly distinguish the locutionary act 'he said that . . .' from the illocutionary act 'he argued that . . .' and the perlocutionary act 'he convinced me that . . .'

It will be seen that the 'consequential effects' here mentioned (see C. *a* and C. *b*) do not include a particular kind of consequential effects, those achieved, e.g., by way of committing the speaker as in promising, which come into the illocutionary act. Perhaps restrictions need making, as there is clearly a difference between what we feel to be the real production of real effects and what we regard as mere conventional consequences; we shall in any case return later to this.

We have here then roughly distinguished three kinds of acts—the locutionary, the illocutionary, and the perlocutionary. Let us make some general comments on these three classes, leaving them still fairly rough. The first three points will be about 'the use of language' again.

(1) Our interest in these lectures is essentially to fasten on the second, illocutionary act and contrast it with the other two. There is a constant tendency in philosophy to elide this in favour of one or other of the other two. Yet it is distinct from both. We have already seen how the expressions 'meaning' and 'use of sentence' can blur the distinction between locutionary and illocutionary acts. We now notice that to speak of the 'use' of language can likewise blur the distinction between the illocutionary and perlocutionary act—so we will distinguish them more carefully in a minute. Speaking of the 'use of "language" for arguing or warning' looks just like speaking of 'the use of "language" for persuading, rousing, alarming'; yet the former may, for rough contrast, be said to be *conventional*, in the sense that at least it could be made explicit by the performative formula; but the latter could not. Thus we can say 'I argue that' or 'I

warn you that' but we cannot say 'I convince you that' or 'I alarm you that'. Further, we may entirely clear up whether someone was arguing or not without touching on the question whether he was convincing anyone or not.

(2) To take this farther, let us be quite clear that the expression 'use of language' can cover other matters even more diverse than the illocutionary and perlocutionary acts and obviously quite diverse from any with which we are here concerned. For example, we may speak of the 'use of language' *for* something, e.g. for joking; and we may use 'in' in a way different from the illocutionary 'in', as when we say 'in saying "p" I was joking' or 'acting a part' or 'writing poetry'; or again we may speak of 'a poetical use of language' as distinct from 'the use of language in poetry'. These references to 'use of language' have nothing to do with the illocutionary act. For example, if I say 'Go and catch a falling star', it may be quite clear what both the meaning and the force of my utterance is, but still wholly unresolved which of these other kinds of things I may be doing. There are aetiolations, parasitic uses, etc., various 'not serious' and 'not full normal' uses. The normal conditions of reference may be suspended, or no attempt made at a standard perlocutionary act, no attempt to make you do anything, as Walt Whitman does not seriously incite the eagle of liberty to soar.

(3) Furthermore, there may be some things we 'do' in some connexion with saying something which do not seem to fall, intuitively at least, exactly into any of these roughly defined classes, or else seem to fall vaguely into

more than one; but any way we do not at the outset feel so clear that they are as remote from our three acts as would be joking or writing poetry. For example, *insinuating*, as when we insinuate something in or by issuing some utterance, seems to involve some convention, as in the illocutionary act; but we cannot *say* 'I insinuate . . .', and it seems like implying to be a clever effect rather than a mere act. A further example is evincing emotion. We may evince emotion in or by issuing an utterance, as when we swear; but once again we have no use here for performative formulas and the other devices of illocutionary acts. We might say that we use swearing[1] *for* relieving our feelings. We must notice that the illocutionary act is a conventional act: an act done as conforming to a convention.

The next three points that arise do so importantly because our acts are *acts*.

(4) Acts of all our three kinds necessitate, since they are the performing of actions, allowance being made for the ills that all action is heir to. We must systematically be prepared to distinguish between 'the act of doing *x*', i.e. achieving *x*, and 'the act of attempting to do *x*'.

In the case of illocutions we must be ready to draw the necessary distinction, not noticed by ordinary language except in exceptional cases, between

(*a*) the act of attempting or purporting (or affecting or professing or claiming or setting up or setting out) to perform a certain illocutionary act, and

---

[1] 'Swearing' is ambiguous: 'I swear by Our Lady' *is* to swear by Our Lady: but 'Bloody' is not to swear by Our Lady.

(*b*) the act of successfully achieving or consummating or bringing off such an act.

This distinction is, or should be, a commonplace of the theory of our language about 'action' in general. But attention has been drawn earlier to its special importance in connexion with performatives: it is always possible, for example, to try to thank or inform somebody yet in different ways to fail, because he doesn't listen, or takes it as ironical, or wasn't responsible for whatever it was, and so on. This distinction will arise, as over any act, over locutionary acts too; but failures here will not be unhappinesses as there, but rather failures to get the words out, to express ourselves clearly, etc.

(5) Since our acts are actions, we must always remember the distinction between producing effects or consequences which are intended or unintended; and (i) when the speaker intends to produce an effect it may nevertheless not occur, and (ii) when he does not intend to produce it or intends not to produce it it may nevertheless occur. To cope with complication (i) we invoke as before the distinction between attempt and achievement; to cope with complication (ii) we invoke the normal linguistic devices of disclaiming (adverbs like 'unintentionally' and so on) which we hold ready for general use in all cases of doing actions.[1]

---

[1] This complication (ii), it may be pointed out, can of course also arise in the cases of both locutionary and illocutionary acts. I may say something or refer to something without meaning to, or commit myself unintentionally to a certain undertaking; for example, I may order someone to do something, when I did not intend to order him to do so. But it is in connexion with perlocution that it is most prominent, as is also the distinction between attempt and achievement.

(6) Furthermore, we must, of course, allow that as actions they may be things that we do not exactly *do*, in the sense that we did them, say, under duress or in any other such way. Other ways besides in which we may not fully do the action are given in (2) above. We may, perhaps, add the cases given in (5) where we produce consequences by mistake, did not intend to do so.

(7) Finally we must meet the objection about our illocutionary and perlocutionary acts—namely that the notion of an act is unclear—by a general doctrine about action. We have the idea of an 'act' as a fixed physical thing that we do, as distinguished from conventions and as distinguished from consequences. But

(*a*) the illocutionary act and even the locutionary act too involve conventions: compare with them the act of doing obeisance. It is obeisance only because it is conventional and it is done only because it is conventional. Compare also the distinction between kicking a wall and kicking a goal;

(*b*) the perlocutionary act always includes some consequences, as when we say 'By doing *x* I was doing *y*': we do bring in a greater or less stretch of 'consequences' always, some of which may be 'unintentional'. There is no restriction to the minimum physical act at all. That we can import an arbitrarily long stretch of what might also be called the 'consequences' of our act into the nomenclature of the act itself is, or should be, a fundamental commonplace of the theory of our language about all 'action' in general. Thus if asked 'What did he do?', we may reply either 'He shot the donkey' or 'He fired a gun' or 'He pulled the trigger' or 'He moved his trigger finger', and all may be correct. So, to shorten the nursery story of the endeavours of the old woman to drive her pig home in time to get her old man's supper, we may in the last resort say that the cat drove or got the pig, or made the pig get, over the stile. If in such cases we *mention* both a B act (illocution) and a C act (perlocution) we shall say '*by* B-ing he C-ed' rather than '*in*-B-ing . . .' This is the reason for calling C a *per*locutionary act as distinct from an illocutionary act.

Next time we shall revert to the distinction between our three kinds of act, and to the expressions 'in' and 'by doing *x* I am doing *y*', with a view to getting the three classes and their members and non-members somewhat clearer. We shall see that just as the locutionary act embraces doing many things at once to be complete, so may the illocutionary and perlocutionary acts.

LECTURE IX

W HEN it was suggested that we embark on a programme of making a list of explicit performative verbs, we ran into some difficulties over the matter of determining whether some utterance was or was not performative, or anyway, *purely* performative. It seemed expedient, therefore, to go back to fundamentals and consider how many senses there may be in which to say something is to do something, or in saying something we do something, or even *by* saying something we do something.

We first distinguished a group of things we do in saying something, which together we summed up by saying we perform a *locutionary act*, which is roughly equivalent to uttering a certain sentence with a certain sense and reference, which again is roughly equivalent to 'meaning' in the traditional sense. Second, we said that we also perform *illocutionary acts* such as informing, ordering, warning, undertaking, &c., i.e. utterances which have a certain (conventional) force. Thirdly, we may also perform *perlocutionary acts*: what we bring about or achieve *by* saying something, such as convincing, persuading, deterring, and even, say, surprising or misleading. Here we have three, if not more, different senses or dimensions of the 'use of a sentence' or of 'the use of language' (and, of course, there are others also). All these three kinds of 'actions' are, simply of course as actions, subject to the usual troubles and reservations about attempt as distinct from achievement, being intentional as distinct from being unintentional, and the like. We then said that we must consider these three kinds of act in greater detail.

We must distinguish the illocutionary from the per-locutionary act: for example we must distinguish 'in saying it I was warning him' from 'by saying it I convinced him, or surprised him, or got him to stop'.

It is the distinction between illocutions and perlocutions which seems likeliest to give trouble, and it is upon this that we shall now embark, taking in the distinction between illocutions and locutions by the way. It is certain that the perlocutionary sense of 'doing an action' must somehow be ruled out as irrelevant to the sense in which an utterance, if the issuing of it is the 'doing of an action', is a performative, at least if that is to be distinct from a constative. For clearly *any*, or almost any, perlocutionary act is liable to be brought off, in sufficiently special circumstances, by the issuing, with or without calculation, of any utterance whatsoever, and in particular by a straightforward constative utterance (if there is such an animal). You may, for example, deter me (C. *b*)[1] from doing something by informing me, perhaps guilelessly yet opportunely, what the consequences of doing it would in fact be: and this applies even to

[1] See p. 102 for the significance of these references.

(C. *a*)[1] for you may convince me (C. *a*)[1] that she is an adulteress by asking her whether it was not her hand-kerchief which was in *X's* bedroom,[2] or by stating that it was hers.

We have then to draw the line between an action we do (here an illocution) and its consequences. Now in general, and if the action is not one of saying something but a non-conventional 'physical' action, this is an intricate matter. As we have seen, we can, or may like to think we can, class, by stages, more and more of what is initially and ordinarily included or possibly might be included under the name given to 'our act' itself[3] as *really* only *consequences*, however little remote and however naturally to be anticipated, of our actual action in the supposed minimum physical sense, which will then transpire to be

---

[1] See p. 102 for the significance of these references.

[2] That the giving of straightforward information produces, almost always, consequential effects upon action, is no more surprising than the converse, that the doing of any action (including the uttering of a per-formative) has regularly the consequence of making ourselves and others aware of facts. To do any act in a perceptible or detectable way is to afford ourselves and generally others also the opportunity of coming to know both (*a*) that we did it, and further (*b*) many other facts as to our motives, our character or what not which may be inferred from our having done it. If you hurl a tomato at a political meeting (or bawl 'I protest' when someone else does—if that is performing an action) the consequence will probably be to make others aware that you object, and to make them think that you hold certain political beliefs: but this will not make either the throw or the shout true or false (though they may be, even deliberately, misleading). And by the same token, the production of any number of consequential effects will not prevent a constative utterance from *being* true or false.

[3] I do not here go into the question how far consequences may extend. The usual errors on this topic may be found in, for example, Moore's *Principia Ethica*.

the making of some movement or movements with parts of our body (e.g. crooking our finger, which produced a movement of the trigger, which produced . . . which produced the death of the donkey). There is, of course, much to be said about this which need not concern us here. But at least in the case of acts of saying something,

(1) *nomenclature* affords us an assistance which it generally withholds in the case of 'physical' actions. For with physical actions we nearly always naturally name the action *not* in terms of what we are here calling the minimum physical act, but in terms which embrace a greater or less but indefinitely extensive range of what might be called its natural consequences (or, looking at it another way, the intention with which it was done).

We not merely do not use the notion of a minimum physical act (which is in any case doubtful) but we do not seem to have any class of names which distinguish physical acts from consequences: whereas with acts of saying something, the vocabulary of names for acts (B) seems expressly designed to mark a break at a certain regular point between the act (our saying something) and its consequences (which are usually not the *saying* of anything), or at any rate a great many of them.[1]

---

[1] Note that if we suppose the minimum physical act to be movement of the body when we say 'I moved my finger', the fact that the object moved *is* part of my body does in fact introduce a new sense of 'moved'. Thus I may be able to waggle my ears as a schoolboy does, or by grasping them between my finger and thumb, or move my foot either in the ordinary way or by manipulating with my hand when I have pins and needles. The ordinary use of 'move' in such examples as 'I moved my

(2) Furthermore, we seem to derive some assistance from the special nature of acts of saying something by contrast with ordinary physical actions: for with these latter even the minimum physical action, which we are seeking to detach from its consequences, is, being a bodily movement, *in pari materia*[1] with at least many of its immediate and natural consequences, whereas, whatever the immediate and natural consequences of an act of saying something may be, they are at least not normally other further acts of saying something, whether more particularly on the speaker's own part or even on the part of others.[2] So that we have here a sort of regular natural break in the chain, which is wanting in the case of physical actions, and which is associated with the special class of names for illocutions.

This may get us some little way, but, it may be asked at this point, are not the consequences imported with the nomenclature of perlocutions really consequences of the acts (A), the locutions? Ought we not, in seeking to

finger' is ultimate. We must not seek to go back behind it to 'pulling on my muscles' and the like.

[1] This *in pari materia* could be misleading to you. I do not mean, as was pointed out in the previous footnote, that my 'moving my finger' is, metaphysically, in the least like 'the trigger moving' which is its consequence, or like 'my finger's moving the trigger'. But 'a movement of a trigger finger' is *in pari materia* with 'a movement of a trigger'.

Or we could put the matter in a most important other way by saying that the sense in which saying something produces effects on other persons, or *causes* things, is a fundamentally different sense of cause from that used in physical causation by pressure, &c. It has to operate through the conventions of language and is a matter of influence exerted by one person on another: this is probably the original sense of 'cause'.

[2] See below.

detach 'all' consequences, to go right back beyond the illocution to the locution—and indeed to the act (A. *a*), the uttering of noises, which is a physical movement?[1] It has, of course, been admitted that to perform an illocutionary act is necessarily to perform a locutionary act: that, for example, to congratulate is necessarily to say certain words; and to say certain words is necessarily, at least in part, to make certain more or less indescribable movements with the vocal organs.[2] So that the divorce between 'physical' actions and acts of saying something is not in all ways complete—there is some connexion. But (i) while this may be important in some connexions and contexts, it does not seem to prevent the drawing of *a* line for our present purposes where we want one, that is, between the completion of the illocutionary act and all consequences thereafter. And further (ii), much more important, we must avoid the idea, suggested above though not stated, that the illocutionary act is a *consequence* of the locutionary act, and even the idea that what is imported by the nomenclature of illocutions is an *additional* reference to *some* of the consequences of the locutions,[3] i.e. that to say 'he urged me to' is to say that he said certain words and in addition that his saying them had *or* perhaps was intended to have certain conse-

---

[1] Or is it? We have already noted that 'production of noises' is itself really a consequence of the minimum physical act of moving one's vocal organs.

[2] Still confining ourselves, for simplicity, to *spoken* utterance.

[3] Though see below.

quences (? an effect upon me). We should not, if we were to insist for some reason and in some sense on 'going back' from the illocution to the phonetic act (A. *a*), be going back to a minimum physical action via the chain of its consequences, in the way that we supposedly go back from the death of the rabbit to the movement of the trigger finger. The uttering of noises may be a consequence (physical) of the movement of the vocal organs, the breath, &c.: but the uttering of a word is *not* a consequence of the uttering of a noise, whether physical or otherwise. Nor is the uttering of words with a certain meaning a *consequence* of uttering the words, whether physical or otherwise. For that matter, even phatic (A. *b*) and rhetic (A. *c*) acts are not *consequences*, let alone physical consequences, of phonetic acts (A. *a*). What we do import by the use of the nomenclature of illocution is a reference, not to the consequences (at least in any ordinary sense) of the locution, but to the conventions of illocutionary force as bearing on the special circumstances of the occasion of the issuing of the utterance. We shall shortly return to the senses in which the successful or consummated performance of an illocutionary act *does* bring in 'consequences' or 'effects' in certain senses.[1]

[1] We may still feel tempted to ascribe some 'primacy' to the locution as against the illocution, seeing that, given some individual rhetic act (A. *c*), there may yet be room for doubt as to how it should be described in the nomenclature of illocutions. Why after all should we label one *A* the other *B*? We may agree on the actual words that were uttered, and even also on the senses in which they were being used and on the realities

I have so far argued, then, that we can have hopes of isolating the illocutionary act from the perlocutionary as producing consequences, and that it is not itself a 'consequence' of the locutionary act. Now, however, I must point out that the illocutionary act as distinct from the perlocutionary is connected with the production of effects in certain senses:

(1) Unless a certain effect is achieved, the illocutionary act will not have been happily, successfully performed. This is not to say that the illocutionary act is the achieving of a certain effect. I cannot be said to have warned an audience unless it hears what I say and takes what I say in a certain sense. An effect must be achieved on the audience if the illocutionary act is to be carried out.

to which they were being used to refer, and yet still disagree as to whether, in the circumstances, they amounted to an order or a threat or merely to advice or a warning. Yet after all, there is ample room, equally, for disagreement in individual cases as to how the rhetic act (A. *c*) should be described in the nomenclature of locutions (What did he really mean? To what person, time, or what not was he actually referring?): and indeed, we may often agree that his act was definitely one say, of ordering (illocution), while yet uncertain what it was he was meaning to order (locution). It is plausible to suppose that the act is at least as much 'bound' to be describable as some more or less *definite* type of illocution as it is to be describable as some more or less definite locutionary act (A). Difficulties about conventions and intentions must arise in deciding upon the correct description whether of a locution or of an illocution: deliberate, or unintentional, ambiguity of meaning or reference is perhaps as common as deliberate or unintentional failure to make plain 'how our words are to be taken' (in the illocutionary sense). Moreover, the whole apparatus of 'explicit performatives' (see above) serves to obviate disagreements as to the description of illocutionary acts. It is much harder in fact to obviate disagreements as to the description of 'locutionary acts'. Each, however, is conventional and liable to have a 'construction' put on it by judges.

How should we best put it here? And how can we limit it? Generally the effect amounts to bringing about the understanding of the meaning and of the force of the locution. So the performance of an illocutionary act involves the securing of *uptake*.

(2) The illocutionary act 'takes effect' in certain ways, as distinguished from producing consequences in the sense of bringing about states of affairs in the 'normal' way, i.e. changes in the natural course of events. Thus 'I name this ship the *Queen Elizabeth*' has the effect of naming or christening the ship; then certain subsequent acts such as referring to it as the *Generalissimo Stalin* will be out of order.

(3) We have said that many illocutionary acts invite by convention a response or sequel. Thus an order invites the response of obedience and a promise that of fulfilment. The response or sequel may be 'one-way' or 'two-way': thus we may distinguish arguing, ordering, promising, suggesting, and asking to, from offering, asking whether you will and asking 'Yes or no?' If this response is accorded, or the sequel implemented, that requires a second act by the speaker or another person; and it is a commonplace of the consequence-language that this cannot be included under the initial stretch of action.

Generally we can, however, always say 'I got him to' with such a word. This does make the act one ascribed to me and it is, when words are or may be employed, a perlocutionary act. Thus we must distinguish 'I ordered him and he obeyed' from 'I *got him* to obey'. The general implication of the latter is that other additional means were employed to produce this consequence as ascribable to me, inducements, personal presence, and influence which may amount to duress; there is even very often an illocutionary act distinct from merely ordering, as when I say 'I got him to do it by stating *x*'.

So here are three ways, securing uptake, taking effect, and inviting a response, in which illocutionary acts are bound up with effects; and these are all distinct from the producing of effects which is characteristic of the perlocutionary act.

The perlocutionary act may be either the achievement of a perlocutionary object (convince, persuade) or the production of a perlocutionary sequel. Thus the act of warning may achieve its perlocutionary object of alerting and also have the perlocutionary sequel of alarming, and and an argument against a view may fail to achieve its object but have the perlocutionary sequel of convincing our opponent of its truth ('I only succeeded in convincing him'). What is the perlocutionary object of one illocution may be the sequel of another. For example, warning may produce the sequel of deterring and saying 'Don't', whose object is to deter, may produce the sequel of alerting or even alarming. Some perlocutionary acts are always the producing of a sequel, namely those where there is no illocutionary formula: thus I may surprise you or upset you or humiliate you by a locution, though there is no illocutionary formula 'I surprise you by . . .', 'I upset you by . . .', 'I humiliate you by . . .'

It is characteristic of perlocutionary acts that the response achieved, or the sequel, can be achieved additionally or entirely by non-locutionary means: thus intimidation may be achieved by waving a stick or pointing a gun. Even in the cases of convincing, persuading, getting to obey and getting to believe, we may achieve the response non-verbally; but if there is no illocutionary act, it is doubtful whether this language characteristic of perlocutionary objects should be used. Compare the use of 'got him to' with that of 'got him to obey'. However, this alone is not enough to distinguish illocutionary acts, since we can for example warn or order or appoint or give or protest or apologize by non-verbal means and these are illocutionary acts. Thus we may cock a snook or hurl a tomato by way of protest.

More important is the question whether these responses and sequels can be achieved by non-conventional means. Certainly we can achieve the same perlocutionary sequels by non-conventional means (or as we say 'unconventional' means), means that are not conventional at all or not for that purpose; thus I may persuade some one by gently swinging a big stick or gently mentioning that his aged parents are still in the Third Reich. Strictly speaking, there cannot be an illocutionary act unless the means employed are conventional, and so the means for achieving it non-verbally must be conventional. But it is difficult to say where conventions begin and end; thus I may warn him by swinging a stick or I may give him something by merely handing it to him. But if I warn him by swinging a stick, then swinging my stick is a warning: he would know very well what I meant: it may seem an unmistakable threatening gesture. Similar difficulties arise over giving tacit consent to some arrangement, or promising tacitly, or voting by a show of hands. But the fact remains that many illocutionary acts cannot be performed except by saying something. This is true of stating, informing (as distinct from showing), arguing, giving estimates, reckoning, and finding (in the legal sense); it is true of the great majority of verdictives and expositives as opposed to many exercitives and commissives.[1]

[1] [For the definition of verdictives, expositives, exercitives, and commissives see Lecture XII.—J.O.U.]

LECTURE X

FORGETTING for the time the initial distinction between performatives and constatives and the programme of finding a list of explicit performative words, notably verbs, we made a fresh start by considering the senses in which to say something is to do something. Thus we distinguished the locutionary act (and within it the phonetic, the phatic, and the rhetic acts) which has a *meaning*; the illocutionary act which has a certain *force* in saying something; the perlocutionary act which is *the achieving of* certain *effects* by saying something.

We distinguished in the last lecture some senses of consequences and effects in these connexions, especially three senses in which effects can come in even with illocutionary acts, namely, securing uptake, taking effect, and inviting responses. In the case of the perlocutionary act we made a rough distinction between achieving an object and producing a sequel. Illocutionary acts are conventional acts: perlocutionary acts are *not* conventional. Acts of *both* kinds can be performed—or, more accurately, acts called by the same name (for example, acts equivalent to the illocutionary act of warning or the perlocutionary act of convincing)—can be brought off non-verbally; but even then to deserve the name of an illocutionary act, for example a warning, it must be a *conventional* non-verbal act: but perlocutionary acts are not conventional, though conventional acts may be made use of in order to bring off the perlocutionary act. A judge should be able to decide, by hearing what was said, what locutionary and illocutionary acts were performed, but not what perlocutionary acts were achieved.

Finally, we have said there is another whole range of questions about 'how we are using language' or 'what we are doing in saying something' which we have said may be, and intuitively seem to be, entirely different—further matters which we are not trenching upon. For example, there are insinuating (and other *non-literal* uses of language), joking (and other *non-serious* uses of language), and swearing and showing off (which are perhaps expressive uses of language). We can say 'In saying *x* I was joking' (insinuating . . ., expressing my feelings, &c.).

We have now to make some final remarks on the formulas:

'In saying *x* I was doing *y*' or 'I did *y*',
'By saying *x* I did *y*' or 'I was doing *y*'.

For it was because of the availability of these formulas which seem specially suitable, the former (*in*) for picking out verbs which are names for illocutionary acts, and the latter (*by*) for picking out verbs which are names for perlocutionary acts, that we chose in fact the names *illocutionary* and *perlocutionary*. Thus, for example:

'*In* saying I would shoot him I was threatening him'.
'*By* saying I would shoot him I alarmed him'.

Will these linguistic formulas provide us with a test for distinguishing illocutionary from perlocutionary acts? They will not. Before I deal with this, though, let me make one general observation or confession. Many of you will be getting impatient at this approach—and to some extent quite justifiably. You will say 'Why not cut the cackle? Why go on about lists available in ordinary talk of names for things we do that have relations to saying, and about formulas like the "in" and "by" formulas? Why not get down to discussing the thing bang off in terms of linguistics and psychology in a straightforward fashion? Why be so devious?' Well, of course, I agree that this will have to be done—only I say *after*, not before, seeing what we can screw out of ordinary language even if in what comes out there is a strong element of the undeniable. Otherwise we shall overlook things and go too fast.

'In' and 'by' are anyway worth investigation; for that matter, so are 'when', 'while', &c. The importance of these investigations is obvious in the general question of how the various possible descriptions of 'what I do' are interrelated, as we have seen in the matter of 'consequences'. We turn, then, to the 'in' and 'by' formulas, and after that shall turn back again to our initial distinction of the performative and constative, to see how it fares in this newly provided framework.

We will take first the formula: 'In saying x I was doing y' (or 'I did y').

(1) Its use is not confined to illocutionary acts; it will apply (*a*) with locutionary acts and (*b*) with acts which seem to fall outside our classification altogether. It certainly is not the case that if we can say 'in saying *x* you were *y*-ing', then 'to *y*' is necessarily to perform an illocutionary act. At most it might be claimed that the formula will not suit the perlocutionary act, while the 'by' formula will not suit the illocutionary act. In particular (*a*) we use the same formula where 'to *y*' is to perform an incidental part of a locutionary act: for example, 'In saying I detested Catholics, I was referring only to the present day', or, 'I was meaning or thinking of *Roman* Catholics'. Though in this case we would perhaps more commonly use the formula 'in speaking of'. Another example of this kind is: 'In saying "Iced ink" I was uttering the noises "I stink".' But besides this there are (*b*) other apparently miscellaneous cases, such as 'In saying *x* you were making a mistake' or 'failing to observe a necessary distinction' or 'breaking the law', or 'running a risk', or 'forgetting': to make a mistake or to run a risk is certainly not to perform an illocutionary act, nor even a locutionary one.

We may attempt to get out of (*a*), the fact that it is not confined to illocutionary acts, by arguing that 'saying' is ambiguous. Where the use is not illocutionary 'saying' could be replaced by 'speaking of', or 'using the expression', or instead of 'in saying *x*' we could say 'by the word *x*' or 'in using the word *x*'. This is the sense of 'saying' in which it is followed by inverted commas, and in such cases we refer to the phatic and not the rhetic act.

The case (*b*), of miscellaneous acts falling outside our classification, is more difficult. A possible test would be the following: where we can put the *y*-verb[1] into a non-continuous tense (preterite or present) instead of the continuous tense, or equally where we can change the 'in' into 'by' while keeping the continuous tense, then the *y*-verb is not the name for an illocution. Thus, for 'In saying that he was making a mistake', we could put, without change of sense, either 'In saying that he made a mistake' or 'By saying that he was making a mistake': but we do not say 'In saying that I protested' nor 'By saying that I was protesting'.

(2) But on the whole we might claim that the formula does not go with perlocutionary verbs like 'convinced', 'persuaded', 'deterred'. But we must qualify this a little. First, exceptions arise through the incorrect use of language. Thus people say 'Are you intimidating me?' instead of 'threatening', and thus might say 'In saying *x*, he was intimidating me'. Second, the same word may genuinely be used in both illocutionary and perlocutionary ways. For example, 'tempting' is a verb which may easily be used in either way. We don't have 'I tempt you to' but we do have 'Let me tempt you to', and exchanges like 'Do have another whack of ice-cream'—'Are you tempting me?'. The last question

---

[1] [That is, the verb substituted for '*y*' in 'In saying *x* I was *y*-ing'. J.O.U.]

would be absurd in a perlocutionary sense, since it would be one for the speaker to answer, if anyone. If I say 'Oh, why not?' it seems that I am tempting him, but he may not really be tempted. Third, there is the proleptic use of verbs such as, for example, 'seducing' or 'pacifying'. In this case 'trying to' seems always a possible addition with a perlocutionary verb. But we cannot say that the illocutionary verb is always equivalent to trying to do something which might be expressed by a perlocutionary verb, as for example that 'argue' is equivalent to 'try to convince', or 'warn' is equivalent to 'try to alarm' or 'alert'. For firstly, the distinction between doing and trying to do is already there in the illocutionary verb as well as in the perlocutionary verb; we distinguish arguing from trying to argue as well as convincing from trying to convince. Further, many illocutionary acts are not cases of trying to do any perlocutionary act; for example, to promise is not to try to do anything.

But we may still ask whether we may possibly use 'in' with the perlocutionary act; this is tempting when the act is not intentionally achieved. But even here it is probably incorrect, and we should use 'by'. Or at any rate, if I say, for example, 'In saying *x* I was convincing him', I am here accounting not for how I came to be saying *x* but for how I came to be convincing him; this is the other way round from the use of the formula in explaining what we meant by a phrase when we used the 'in saying' formula, and involves another sense ('in the process' or 'in the course of' as distinct from 'a criterion') from its use with illocutionary verbs.

Let us now consider the general meaning of the 'in' formula. If I say 'In doing *A* I was doing *B*', I may mean either that *A* involves *B* (*A* accounts for *B*) or that *B* involves *A* (*B* accounts for *A*). This distinction may be brought out by contrasting (α 1) 'In the course or process of doing *A*, I was doing *B*' (in building a house, I was building a wall) and (α 2) 'In doing *A*, I was in the course or process of doing *B*' (in building a wall I was building a house). Or again, contrast (α 1): 'In uttering the noises *N* I was saying *S*' and (α 2): 'In saying *S* I was uttering the noises *N*'; in (α 1) I account for *A* (here, my uttering the noises) and state my purpose in uttering the noises, whereas in (α 2) I account for *B* (my uttering the noises) and thus state the effect of my uttering the noises. The formula is often used to account for my doing something in answer to the question: 'How come you were doing so-and-so?' Of the two different emphases, the Dictionary prefers the former case (α 1), in which we account for *B*, but we equally often use it as in case (α 2), to account for *A*.

If we now consider the example:

In saying . . . I was forgetting . . .,

we find that *B* (forgetting) explains how we came to say it, i.e. it accounts for *A*. Similarly

In buzzing I was thinking that butterflies buzzed accounts for my buzzing (*A*). This seems to be the use of

the 'in saying' formula when used with locutionary
verbs; it accounts for my saying what I did (and not
for my meaning).

But if we consider the examples:

(α 3) In buzzing, I was pretending to be a bee,
    In buzzing I was behaving like a buffoon,

we find here that saying what one did (buzzing) in
intention or in fact constituted my saying so-and-so, an
act of a certain kind, and made it callable by a different
name. The illocutionary example:

In saying so-and-so I was warning

is of this kind: it is not of either of the 'in the course of'
kinds (α 1) and (α 2) (where A accounts for B or vice
versa). But it is different from the locutionary examples,
in that the act is constituted not by intention or by fact,
essentially but by *convention* (which is, of course, a
fact). These features serve to pick out illocutionary acts
most satisfactorily.[1]

When the 'in saying' formula is used with perlocutionary verbs, on the other hand, it is used in an 'in
the process of' sense (α 1), but it accounts for B, whereas the locutionary verb case accounts for A. So it is
different from both the locutionary and the illocutionary
cases.

---

[1] But suppose there is a quack dentist. We can say 'In inserting the
plate he was practising dentistry.' There is a convention here just as in
the warning case—a judge could decide.

The question 'How come?' is not confined to questions of means and ends, we may observe. Thus in the example:

In saying A . . . I was forgetting B

we account for A, but in a new sense of 'accounts for' or 'involves', which is not that of means and end. Again, in the example:

In saying . . . I was convincing . . . (was humiliating . . .),

we account for B (my convincing or humiliating him) which is indeed a consequence but is not a consequence of a means.

The 'by' formula is likewise not confined to perlocutionary verbs. There is the locutionary use (by saying . . . I meant . . .), the illocutionary use (by saying . . . I was thereby warning . . .) and a variety of miscellaneous uses (by saying . . . I put myself in the wrong). The uses of 'by' are at least two in general:

(*a*) By hitting the nail on the head I was driving it into the wall,

(*b*) By inserting a plate, I was practising dentistry.

In (*a*) 'by' indicates the means by which, the manner in which or the method by which I was bringing off the action; in (*b*) 'by' indicates a criterion, that about what I did which enables my action to be classified as practising dentistry. There seems little difference between the two cases except that the use to indicate a criterion seems more external. This second sense of 'by'—the criterion sense—is, it seems, also very close to 'in' in one of its senses: 'In saying that I was breaking the law (broke the law)'; and in this way 'by' can certainly be used with illocutionary verbs in the 'by saying' formula. Thus we may say 'By saying . . . I was warning him (I warned him)'. But 'by', in this sense, is not used with perlocutionary verbs. If I say 'By saying . . . I convinced (persuaded) him', 'by' will here have the means-to-end sense, or anyway signify the manner in which or method by which I did it. Is the 'by'-formula ever used in 'means-to-end sense' with an illocutionary verb? It would seem that it is in at least two kinds of cases:

(*a*) When we adopt a verbal means of doing something instead of a non-verbal means, when we talk instead of using a stick. Thus in the example: 'By saying "I do" I was marrying her', the performative 'I do' is a means to the end of marriage. Here 'saying' is used in the sense in which it takes inverted commas and is using words or language, a phatic and not a rhetic act.

(*b*) When one performative utterance is used as an indirect means to perform another act. Thus in the example: 'By saying "I bid three clubs" I informed him that I had no diamonds', I use the performative 'I bid three clubs' as an indirect means to informing him (which is also an illocutionary act).

In sum: to use the 'by saying' formula as a test of an act being perlocutionary, we must first be sure:

(1) that 'by' is being used in an instrumental as distinct from a criterion sense;

(2) that 'saying' is being used

    (*a*) in the full sense of a locutionary act and not a partial sense, for example of a phatic act;

    (*b*) not in the double-convention way as in the example from bridge above.

There are two other subsidiary linguistic tests of the illocutionary act to distinguish it from the perlocutionary:

(1) It seems that in the case of illocutionary verbs we can often say 'To say *x* was to do *y*'. One cannot say 'To hammer the nail was to drive it in' instead of 'By hammering the nail he drove it in'. But this formula will not give us a watertight test, for we can say many things with it; thus we can say 'To say that was to convince him' (a proleptic use?) although 'convince' is a perlocutionary verb.

(2) The verbs that we have classified (intuitively— for that is all we have done so far) as names of illocutionary acts seem to be pretty close to *explicit performative* verbs, for we can say 'I warn you that' and 'I order you to' as explicit performatives; but warning and ordering are illocutionary acts. We can use the performative 'I warn you that' but not 'I convince you that', and can use the performative 'I threaten you with' but not 'I intimidate you by'; convincing and intimidating are perlocutionary acts.

The general conclusion must be, however, that these formulas are at best very slippery tests for deciding whether an expression is an illocution as distinct from a perlocution or neither. But none the less, 'by' and 'in' deserve scrutiny every bit as much as, say, the now-becoming-notorious 'how'.

But what then is the relation between performatives and these illocutionary acts? It seems as though when we have an explicit performative we also have an illocutionary act; let us see, then, what the relationship is between (1) the distinctions made in the earlier lectures regarding performatives and (2) these different kinds of act.

LECTURE XI

WHEN we originally contrasted the performative with the constative utterance we said that

(1) the performative should be doing something as opposed to just saying something; and

(2) the performative is happy or unhappy as opposed to true or false.

Were these distinctions really sound? Our subsequent discussion of doing and saying certainly seems to point to the conclusion that whenever I 'say' anything (except perhaps a mere exclamation like 'damn' or 'ouch') I shall be performing both locutionary and illocutionary acts, and these two kinds of acts seem to be the very things which we tried to use, under the names of 'doing' and 'saying', as a means of distinguishing performatives from constatives. If we are in general always doing both things, how can our distinction survive?

Let us first reconsider the contrast from the side of constative utterances: Of these, we were content to refer to 'statements' as the typical or paradigm case. Would it be correct to say that when we state something

(1) we are doing something as well as and distinct from just saying something, and

(2) our utterance is liable to be happy or unhappy (as well as, if you will, true or false)?

(1) Surely to state is every bit as much to perform an illocutionary act as, say, to warn or to pronounce. Of course it is not to perform an act in some specially physical way, other than in so far as it involves, when verbal, the making of movements of vocal organs; but then nor, as we have seen, is to warn, to protest, to promise or to name. 'Stating' seems to meet all the criteria we had for distinguishing the illocutionary act. Consider such an unexceptionable remark as the following:

> In saying that it was raining, I was not betting or arguing or warning: I was simply stating it as a fact.

Here 'stating' is put absolutely on a level with arguing, betting, and warning. Or again:

> In saying that it was leading to unemployment, I was not warning or protesting: I was simply stating the facts.

Or to take a different type of test also used earlier, surely

> I state that he did not do it

is exactly on a level with

> I argue that he did not do it,
> I suggest that he did not do it,
> I bet that he did not do it, &c.

If I simply use the primary or non-explicit form of utterance:

He did not do it

we may make explicit what we were doing in saying this, or specify the illocutionary force of the utterance, equally by saying any of the above three (or more) things.

Moreover, although the utterance 'He did not do it' is often issued as a statement, and is then undoubtedly true or false (*this* is if anything is), it does not seem possible to say that it differs from 'I state that he did not do it' in this respect. If someone says 'I state that he did not do it', we investigate the truth of his statement in just the same way as if he had said 'He did not do it' *simpliciter*, when we took that to be, as we naturally often should, a statement. That is, to say 'I state that he did not' is to make the very same statement as to say 'He did not': it is not to make a different statement about what 'I' state (except in exceptional cases: the historic and habitual present, &c.). As notoriously, when I say even 'I think he did it' someone is being rude if he says 'That's a statement about you': and this *might* conceivably be about myself, whereas 'I state that he did it' could not. So that there is no necessary conflict between

(*a*) our issuing the utterance being the doing of something,

(*b*) our utterance being true or false.

For that matter compare, for example, 'I warn you that

it is going to charge', where likewise it is both a warning and true or false that it is going to charge; and that comes in in appraising the warning just as much as, though not quite in the same way as, in appraising the statement.

On mere inspection, 'I state that' does not appear to differ in any essential way from 'I maintain that' (to say which is to maintain that), 'I inform you that', 'I testify that', &c. Possibly some 'essential' differences may yet be established between such verbs: but nothing has been done towards this yet.

(2) Moreover, if we think of the second alleged contrast, according to which performatives are happy or unhappy and statements true or false, again from the side of supposed constative utterances, notably statements, we find that statements *are* liable to every kind of infelicity to which performatives are liable. Let us look back again and consider whether statements are not liable to precisely the same disabilities as, say, warnings by way of what we called 'infelicities'—that is various disabilities which make an utterance unhappy without, however, making it true or false.

We have already noted that sense in which saying, as equivalent to stating, 'The cat is on the mat' implies that I believe that the cat is on the mat. This is parallel to the sense—is the same sense—as that in which 'I promise to be there' implies that I intend to be there and that I believe I shall be able to be there. So the statement is liable to the *insincerity* form of infelicity; and even to the *breach* form of infelicity in this sense, that saying or stating that the cat is on the mat commits me to saying or stating 'The mat is underneath the cat' just as much as the performative 'I define X as Y' (in the *fiat* sense say) commits me to using those terms in special ways in future discourse, and we can see how this is connected with such acts as promising. This means that statements can give rise to infelicities of our two $\varGamma$ kinds.

Now what about infelicities of the A and B kinds, which rendered the act—warning, undertaking, &c.—null and void?: can a thing that looks like a statement be null and void just as much as a putative contract? The answer seems to be Yes, importantly. The first cases are A. 1 and A. 2, where there is no convention (or not an accepted convention) or where the circumstances are not appropriate for its invocation by the speaker. Many infelicities of just this type do infect statements.

We have already noticed the case of a putative statement *presupposing* (as it is called) the existence of that which it refers to; if no such thing exists, 'the statement' is not about anything. Now some say that in these circumstances, if, for example, someone asserts that the present King of France is bald, 'the question whether he is bald does not arise'; but it is better to say that the putative statement is null and void, exactly as when I say that I sell you something but it is not mine or (having been burnt) is not any longer in existence. Contracts often are void because the objects they are about do not exist, which involves a breakdown of reference.

But it is important to notice also that 'statements' too are liable to infelicity of this kind in other ways also parallel to contracts, promises, warnings, &c. Just as we often say, for example, 'You cannot order me', in the sense 'You have not the right to order me', which is equivalent to saying that you are not in the appropriate position to do so: so often there are things you cannot state—have no right to state—are not in a position to state. You *cannot* now state how many people there are in the next room; if you say 'There are fifty people in the next room', I can only regard you as guessing or conjecturing (just as sometimes you are not ordering me, which would be inconceivable, but possibly asking me to rather impolitely, so here you are 'hazarding a guess' rather oddly). Here there is something you might, in other circumstances, be in a position to state; but what about statements about other persons' feelings or about the future? Is a forecast or even a prediction about, say, persons' behaviour really a statement? It is important to take the speech-situation as a whole.

Just as sometimes we cannot appoint but only confirm an appointment already made, so sometimes we cannot state but only confirm a statement already made.

Putative statements are also liable to infelicities of type B, flaws, and hitches. Somebody 'says something he did not really mean'—uses the wrong word—says 'the cat is on the mat' when he meant to say 'bat'. Other similar trivialities arise—or rather not entirely trivialities; because it is possible to discuss such utterances entirely in terms of meaning as equivalent to sense and reference and so get confused about them, though they are really easy to understand.

Once we realize that what we have to study is *not* the sentence but the issuing of an utterance in a speech situation, there can hardly be any longer a possibility of not seeing that stating is performing an act. Moreover, comparing stating to what we have said about the illocutionary act, it is an act to which, just as much as to other illocutionary acts, it is essential to 'secure uptake': the doubt about whether I stated something if it was not heard or understood is just the same as the doubt about whether I warned *sotto voce* or protested if someone did not take it as a protest, &c. And statements do 'take effect' just as much as 'namings', say: if I have stated something, then that commits me to other statements: other statements made by me will be in order or out of order. Also some statements or remarks made by you will be henceforward contradicting me or not contradicting me, rebutting me or not rebutting me, and so forth. If perhaps a statement does not invite a response, that is not essential to all illocutionary acts anyway. And certainly in stating we are or may be performing perlocutionary acts of all kinds.

The most that might be argued, and with some plausibility, is that there is no perlocutionary *object* specifically associated with stating, as there is with informing, arguing, &c.; and this comparative purity may be one reason why we give 'statements' a certain special position. But this certainly would not justify giving, say, 'descriptions', if properly used, a similar priority, and it is in any case true of many illocutionary acts.

However, looking at the matter from the side of performatives, we may still feel that they lack something which statements have, even if, as we have shown, the converse is not so. Performatives are, of course, incidentally saying something as well as doing something, but we may feel that they are not essentially true or false as statements are. We may feel that there is here a dimension in which we judge, assess, or appraise the constative utterance (granting as a preliminary that it is felicitous) which does not arise with non-constative or performative utterances. Let us agree that all these circumstances of situation have to be in order for me to have succeeded in stating something, yet when I have, *the* question arises, was what I stated true or false? And this we feel, speaking in popular terms, is now the question of whether the statement 'corresponds with the facts'. With this I agree: attempts to say that the use of the expression 'is true' is equivalent to endorsing or the like are no good. So we have here a new dimension of criticism of the accomplished statement.

But now

(1) doesn't just such a similar objective assessment of the accomplished utterance arise, at least in many cases, with other utterances which seem typically performative; and

(2) is not this account of statements a little over-
     simplified?

First, there is an obvious slide towards truth or falsity
in the case of, for example, verdictives, such as estimat-
ing, finding, and pronouncing. Thus we may:

estimate	rightly or wrongly	for example, that it is half past two,
find	correctly or incorrectly	for example, that he is guilty,
pronounce	correctly or incorrectly	for example, that the bats-man is out.

We shall not say 'truly' in the case of verdictives, but
we shall certainly address ourselves to the same question;
and such adverbs as 'rightly', 'wrongly', 'correctly', and
'incorrectly' are used with statements too.

Or again there is a parallel between inferring and
arguing soundly or validly and stating truly. It is not just
a question of whether he did argue or infer but also of
whether he had a right to, and did he succeed. Warning
and advising may be done correctly or incorrectly, well or
badly. Similar considerations arise about praise, blame,
and congratulation. Blame is not in order, if, say, you
have done the same thing yourself; and the question
always arises whether the praise, blame, or congratulation
was merited or unmerited: it is not enough to say that
you have blamed him and there's an end on't—still one
act is, with reason, preferred to another. The question
whether praise and blame are merited is quite different

from the question whether they are opportune, and the same distinction can be made in the case of advice. It is a different thing to say that advice is good or bad from saying that it is opportune or inopportune, though the timing of advice is more important to its goodness than the timing of blame is to its being merited.

Can we be sure that stating truly is a different *class* of assessment from arguing soundly, advising well, judging fairly, and blaming justifiably? Do these not have something to do in complicated ways with facts? The same is true also of exercitives such as naming, appointing, bequeathing, and betting. Facts come in as well as our knowledge or opinion about facts.

Well, of course, attempts are constantly made to effect this distinction. The soundness of arguments (if they are not deductive arguments which are 'valid') and the meritedness of blame are not objective matters, it is alleged; or in warning, we are told, we should distinguish the 'statement' that the bull is about to charge from the warning itself. But consider also for a moment whether the question of truth or falsity is so very objective. We ask: 'Is it a *fair* statement?', and are the good reasons and good evidence for stating and saying so very different from the good reasons and evidence for performative acts like arguing, warning, and judging? Is the constative, then, always true or false? When a constative is confronted with the facts, we in fact appraise it in ways involving the employment of a vast array of terms which overlap with those that we use in the appraisal of performatives. In real life, as opposed to the simple situations envisaged in logical theory, one cannot always answer in a simple manner whether it is true or false.

Suppose that we confront 'France is hexagonal' with the facts, in this case, I suppose, with France, is it true or false? Well, if you like, up to a point; of course I can see what you mean by saying that it is true for certain intents and purposes. It is good enough for a top-ranking general, perhaps, but not for a geographer. 'Naturally it is pretty rough', we should say, 'and pretty good as a pretty rough statement'. But then someone says: 'But is it true or is it false? I don't mind whether it is rough or not; of course it's rough, but it has to be true or false— it's a statement, isn't it?' How can one answer this question, whether it is true or false that France is hexagonal? It is just rough, and that is the right and final answer to the question of the relation of 'France is hexagonal' to France. It is a rough description; it is not a true or a false one.

Again, in the case of stating truly or falsely, just as much as in the case of advising well or badly, the intents and purposes of the utterance and its context are important; what is judged true in a school book may not be so judged in a work of historical research. Consider the constative, 'Lord Raglan won the battle of Alma', remembering that Alma was a soldier's battle if ever there was one and that Lord Raglan's orders were never transmitted to some of his subordinates. Did Lord Raglan then win the battle of Alma or did he not? Of course in some contexts, perhaps in a school book, it is perfectly justifiable to say so—it is something of an exaggeration, maybe, and there would be no question of giving Raglan a medal for it. As 'France is hexagonal' is rough, so 'Lord Raglan won the battle of Alma' is exaggerated and suitable to some contexts and not to others; it would be pointless to insist on its truth or falsity.

Thirdly, let us consider the question whether it is true that all snow geese migrate to Labrador, given that perhaps one maimed one sometimes fails when migrating to get quite the whole way. Faced with such problems, many have claimed, with much justice, that utterances such as those beginning 'All . . .' are prescriptive definitions or advice to adopt a rule. But what rule? This idea arises partly through not understanding the reference of such statements, which is limited to the known; we cannot quite make the simple statement that the truth of statements depends on facts as distinct from knowledge of facts. Suppose that before Australia is discovered X says 'All swans are white'. If you later find a black swan in Australia, is X refuted? Is his statement false now? Not necessarily: he will take it back but he could say 'I wasn't talking about swans absolutely everywhere; for example, I was not making a statement about possible swans on Mars'. Reference depends on knowledge at the time of utterance.

The truth or falsity of statements is affected by what they leave out or put in and by their being misleading, and so on. Thus, for example, descriptions, which are said to be true or false or, if you like, are 'statements', are surely liable to these criticisms, since they are selective and uttered for a purpose. It is essential to realize that 'true' and 'false', like 'free' and 'unfree', do not stand for anything simple at all; but only for a general dimension of being a right or proper thing to say as opposed to a wrong thing, in these circumstances, to this audience, for these purposes and with these intentions.

In general we may say this: with both statements (and, for example, descriptions) *and* warnings, &c., the question can arise, granting that you had the right to warn and did warn, did state, or did advise, whether you were right to state or warn or advise—not in the sense of whether it was opportune or expedient, but whether, on the facts and your knowledge of the facts and the purposes for which you were speaking, and so on, this was the proper thing to say.

This doctrine is quite different from much that the pragmatists have said, to the effect that the true is what works, &c. The truth or falsity of a statement depends not merely on the meanings of words but on what act you were performing in what circumstances.

What then finally is left of the distinction of the performative and constative utterance? Really we may say that what we had in mind here was this:

(*a*) With the constative utterance, we abstract from the illocutionary (let alone the perlocutionary) aspects of the speech act, and we concentrate on the locutionary: moreover, we use an over-simplified notion of correspondence with the facts—over-simplified because essentially it brings in the illocutionary aspect. This is the ideal of what would be right to say in all circumstances, for any purpose, to any audience, &c. Perhaps it is sometimes realized.

(*b*) With the performative utterance, we attend as much as possible to the illocutionary force of the utterance, and abstract from the dimension of correspondence with facts.

Perhaps neither of these abstractions is so very expedient: perhaps we have here not really two poles, but rather an historical development. Now in certain cases, perhaps with mathematical formulas in physics books as examples of constatives, or with the issuing of simple executive orders or the giving of simple names, say, as examples of performatives, we approximate in real life to finding such things. It was examples of this kind, like 'I apologize', and 'The cat is on the mat', said for no conceivable reason, extreme marginal cases, that gave rise to the idea of two distinct utterances. But the real conclusion must surely be that we need (*a*) to distinguish between locutionary and illocutionary acts, and (*b*) specially and critically to establish with respect to each kind of illocutionary act—warnings, estimates, verdicts, statements, and descriptions—what if any is the specific way in which they are intended, first to be in order or not in order, and second, to be 'right' or 'wrong'; what terms of appraisal and disappraisal are used for each and what they mean. This is a wide field and certainly will not lead to a simple distinction of 'true' and 'false'; nor will it lead to a distinction of statements from the rest, for stating is only one among very numerous speech acts of the illocutionary class.

Furthermore, in general the locutionary act as much as the illocutionary is an abstraction only: every genuine speech act is both. (This is similar to the way in which the phatic act, the rhetic act, &c., are mere abstractions.) But, of course, typically we distinguish different abstracted 'acts' by means of the possible slips between cup and lip, that is, in this case, the different types of nonsense which may be engendered in performing them. We may compare with this point what was said in the opening lecture about the classification of kinds of nonsense.

LECTURE XII

WE have left numerous loose ends, but after a brief résumé we must plough ahead. How did the 'constatives'–'performatives' distinction look in the light of our later theory? In general and for all utterances that we have considered (except perhaps for swearing), we have found:

  (1) Happiness/unhappiness dimension,
 (1*a*) An illocutionary force,
  (2) Truth/falsehood dimension,
 (2*a*) A locutionary meaning (sense and reference).

The doctrine of the performative/constative distinction stands to the doctrine of locutionary and illocutionary acts in the total speech act as the *special* theory to the *general* theory. And the need for the general theory arises simply because the traditional 'statement' is an abstraction, an ideal, and so is its traditional truth or falsity. But on this point I could do no more than explode a few hopeful fireworks. In particular, the following morals are among those I wanted to suggest:

(A) The total speech act in the total speech situation is the *only actual* phenomenon which, in the last resort, we are engaged in elucidating.

(B) Stating, describing, &c., are *just two* names among

a very great many others for illocutionary acts; they have no unique position.

(C) In particular, they have no unique position over the matter of being related to facts in a unique way called being true or false, because truth and falsity are (except by an artificial abstraction which is always possible and legitimate for certain purposes) not names for relations, qualities, or what not, but for a dimension of assessment—how the words stand in respect of satisfactoriness to the facts, events, situations, &c., to which they refer.

(D) By the same token, the familiar contrast of 'normative or evaluative' as opposed to the factual is in need, like so many dichotomies, of elimination.

(E) We may well suspect that the theory of 'meaning' as equivalent to 'sense and reference' will certainly require some weeding-out and reformulating in terms of the distinction between locutionary and illocutionary acts (*if these notions are sound*: they are only adumbrated here). I admit that not enough has been done here: I have taken the old 'sense and reference' on the strength of current views. But here we should consider again the statement which we have called 'void' for breakdown of reference, e.g., the statement 'John's children are all bald' if made when John has no children.

Now we said that there was one further thing obviously requiring to be done, which is a matter of prolonged fieldwork. We said long ago that we needed a list of 'explicit performative verbs'; but in the light of the more

general theory we now see that what we need is a list of
illocutionary forces of an utterance. The old distinction,
however, between *primary* and *explicit* will survive the
sea-change from the performative/constative distinction
to the theory of speech-acts quite successfully. For we
have since seen reason to suppose that the sorts of test
suggested for the explicit performative verbs ('to say . . .
is to . . .', &c.) will do, and in fact do better for sorting out
those verbs which make explicit, as we shall now say, the
illocutionary force of an utterance, or what illocutionary
act it is that we are performing in issuing that utterance.
What will *not* survive the transition, unless perhaps as a
marginal limiting case, and hardly surprisingly because it
gave trouble from the start, is the notion of the purity of
performatives: this was essentially based upon a belief
in the dichotomy of performatives and constatives, which
we see has to be abandoned in favour of more general
families of related and overlapping speech acts, which are
just what we have now to attempt to classify.

Using then the simple test (with caution) of the first
person singular present indicative active form, and
going through the dictionary (a concise one should do)
in a liberal spirit, we get a list of verbs of the order
of the third power of 10.[1] I said I would attempt some
general preliminary classification and make some remarks on these proposed classes. Well, here we go. I

---

[1] Why use this expression instead of 1,000? First, it looks impressive
and scientific; second, because it goes from 1,000 to 9,999—a good
margin—whereas the other might be taken to mean 'about 1,000'—too
narrow a margin.

shall only give you a run around, or rather a flounder around.

I distinguish five very general classes: but I am far from equally happy about all of them. They are, however, quite enough to play Old Harry with two fetishes which I admit to an inclination to play Old Harry with, viz. (1) the true/false fetish, (2) the value/fact fetish. I call then these classes of utterance, classified according to their illocutionary force, by the following more-or-less rebarbative names:

(1) Verdictives.
(2) Exercitives.
(3) Commissives.
(4) Behabitives (a shocker this).
(5) Expositives.

We shall take them in order, but first I will give a rough idea of each.

The first, verdictives, are typified by the giving of a verdict, as the name implies, by a jury, arbitrator, or umpire. But they need not be final; they may be, for example, an estimate, reckoning, or appraisal. It is essentially giving a finding as to something—fact, or value—which is for different reasons hard to be certain about.

The second, exercitives, are the exercising of powers, rights, or influence. Examples are appointing, voting, ordering, urging, advising, warning, &c.

The third, commissives, are typified by promising or otherwise undertaking; they *commit* you to doing something, but include also declarations or announcements of intention, which are not promises, and also rather vague things which we may call espousals, as for example, siding with. They have obvious connexions with verdictives and exercitives.

The fourth, behabitives, are a very miscellaneous group, and have to do with attitudes and *social behaviour*. Examples are apologizing, congratulating, commending, condoling, cursing, and challenging.

The fifth, expositives, are difficult to define. They make plain how our utterances fit into the course of an argument or conversation, how we are using words, or, in general, are expository. Examples are 'I reply', 'I argue', 'I concede', 'I illustrate', 'I assume', 'I postulate'. We should be clear from the start that there are still wide possibilities of marginal or awkward cases, or of overlaps.

The last two classes are those which I find most troublesome, and it could well be that they are not clear or are cross-classified, or even that some fresh classification altogether is needed. I am not putting any of this forward as in the very least definitive. Behabitives are troublesome because they seem too miscellaneous altogether: and expositives because they are enormously numerous and important, and seem both to be included in the other classes and at the same time to be unique in a way that I have not succeeded in making clear even to myself. It could well be said that all aspects are present in all my classes.

1. VERDICTIVES

Examples are:

acquit	convict	find (as a matter of fact)
hold (as a matter of law)	interpret as	understand
read it as	rule	calculate
reckon	estimate	locate
place	date	measure
put it at	make it	take it
grade	rank	rate
assess	value	describe
characterize	diagnose	analyse

Further examples are found in appraisals or assessments of character, such as 'I should call him industrious'.

Verdictives consist in the delivering of a finding, official or unofficial, upon evidence or reasons as to value or fact, so far as these are distinguishable. A verdictive is a judicial act as distinct from legislative or executive acts, which are both exercitives. But some judicial acts, in the wider sense that they are done by judges instead of for example, juries, really are exercitive. Verdictives have obvious connexions with truth and falsity, soundness and unsoundness and fairness and unfairness. That the content of a verdict is true or false is shown, for example, in a dispute over an umpire's calling 'Out', 'Three strikes', or 'Four balls'.

Comparison with exercitives

As official acts, a judge's ruling makes law; a jury's finding makes a convicted felon; an umpire's giving the batsman out, or calling a fault or a no-ball, makes the batsman out, the service a fault, or the ball a no-ball. It is done in virtue of an official position: but it still purports to be correct or incorrect, right or wrong, justifiable or unjustifiable on the evidence. It is not made as a decision in favour or against. The judicial act is, if you like, executive, but we must distinguish the executive utterance, 'You shall have it', from the verdict, 'It is yours', and must similarly distinguish the assessing from the awarding of damages.

Comparison with commissives

Verdictives have an effect, in the law, on ourselves and on others. The giving of a verdict or an estimate does, for example, commit us to certain future conduct, in the sense that any speech-act does and perhaps more so, at least to consistency, and maybe we know to what it will commit us. Thus to give a certain verdict will commit us or, as we say, commits us, to awarding damages. Also, by an interpretation of the facts we may commit ourselves to a certain verdict or estimate. To give a verdict may very well be to espouse also; it may commit us to standing up for someone, defending him, &c.

Comparison with behabitives

To congratulate may imply a verdict about value or

character. Again, in one sense of 'blame' which is equivalent to 'hold responsible', to blame is a verdictive, but in another sense it is to adopt an attitude towards a person and is thus a behabitive.

Comparison with expositives

When I say 'I interpret', 'I analyse', 'I describe', 'I characterize', this, in a way, is to give a verdict, but is essentially connected with verbal matters and clarifying our exposition. 'I call you out' must be distinguished from 'I call that "out"'; the first is a verdict *given* the use of words, like 'I should describe that as cowardly'; the second is a verdict *about* the use of words, as 'I should describe that as "cowardly"'.

2. EXERCITIVES

An exercitive is the giving of a decision in favour of or against a certain course of action, or advocacy of it. It is a decision that something is to be so, as distinct from a judgement that it is so: it is advocacy that it should be so, as opposed to an estimate that it is so; it is an award as opposed to an assessment; it is a sentence as opposed to a verdict. Arbitrators and judges make use of exercitives as well as issuing verdictives. Its consequences may be that others are 'compelled' or 'allowed' or 'not allowed' to do certain acts.

It is a very wide class; examples are:

appoint	degrade	demote
dismiss	excommunicate	name

order	command	direct
sentence	fine	grant
levy	vote for	nominate
choose	claim	give
bequeath	pardon	resign
warn	advise	plead
pray	entreat	beg
urge	press	recommend
proclaim	announce	quash
countermand	annul	repeal
enact	reprieve	veto
dedicate	declare closed	declare open

Comparison with verdictives

'I hold', 'I interpret', and the like, may, if official, be exercitive acts. In that case one may well say 'I shall interpret' and this is a goodish test of whether we have a verdictive or exercitive. Furthermore, 'I award' and 'I absolve' are exercitives, which will be based on verdicts.

Comparison with commissives

Many exercitives such as *permit*, *authorize*, *depute*, *offer*, *concede*, *give*, *sanction*, *stake*, and *consent* do in fact commit one to a course of action. If I say 'I declare war' or 'I disown', the whole purpose of my act is to commit me personally to a certain course of action. The connexion between an exercitive and committing oneself is as close as that between meaning and implication. It is obvious that appointing and naming do commit us, but we would rather say that they confer powers, rights, names, &c., or change or eliminate them.

Comparison with behabitives

Such exercitives as 'I challenge', 'I protest', 'I approve', are closely connected with behabitives. Challenging, protesting, approving, commending, and recommending, may be the taking up of an attitude or the performing of an act.

Comparison with expositives

Such exercitives as 'I withdraw', 'I demur', and 'I object', when used in the context of argument or conversation, may be regarded as expositives.

Typical contexts in which exercitives are used are in:

(1) filling offices and appointments, candidatures, elections, admissions, resignations, dismissals, and applications,
(2) advice, exhortation, and petition,
(3) enablements, orders, sentences, and annulments,
(4) the conduct of meetings and business,
(5) rights, claims, accusations, &c.

3. COMMISSIVES

The whole point of a commissive is to commit the speaker to a certain course of action. Examples are:

promise	covenant	contract
undertake	bind myself	give my word

am determined to	intend	declare my intention
mean to	plan	purpose
propose to	shall	contemplate
envisage	engage	swear
guarantee	pledge myself	bet
vow	agree	consent
dedicate myself to	declare for	side with
adopt	champion	embrace
espouse	oppose	favour

Declarations of intention differ from undertakings, and it might be questioned whether they should be classed together. As we have a distinction between urging and ordering, so we have a distinction between intending and promising. But both are covered by the primary performative 'shall'; thus we have the locutions 'shall probably', 'shall do my best to', 'shall very likely'.

There is also a slide towards 'descriptives'. At the one extreme I may *just* state that I have an intention, but I may also declare or express or announce my intention or determination. 'I declare my intention' undoubtedly does commit me; and to say 'I intend' is generally to declare or announce. The same thing happens with espousals, as, for example, in 'I dedicate my life to . . .'. In the case of commissives like 'favour', 'oppose', 'adopt the view', 'take the view', and 'embrace', you cannot state that you favour, oppose, &c., generally, without announcing that you do so. To say 'I favour X' may, according to context, be to *vote* for X, to *espouse* X, or to *applaud* X.

Comparison with verdictives

Verdictives commit us to actions in two ways:

(*a*) to those necessary for consistency with and support of our verdict,

(*b*) to those that may be, or may be involved in, the consequences of a verdict.

Comparison with exercitives

Exercitives commit us to the consequences of an act, for example of naming. In the special case of permissives we might ask whether they should be classified as exercitives or as commissives.

Comparison with behabitives

Reactions such as resenting, applauding, and commending do involve espousing and committing ourselves in the way that advice and choice do. But behabitives commit us to *like* conduct, by implication, and not to that actual conduct. Thus if I blame, I adopt an attitude to someone else's past conduct, but can commit myself only to avoiding like conduct.

Comparison with expositives

Swearing, promising, and guaranteeing that something is the case work like expositives, as, for example, when you give your word that you have done, not that you will do, something. Calling, defining, analysing, and assuming form one group, and supporting, agreeing, disagreeing, maintaining, and defending form another group of illocutions which seem to be both expositive and commissive.

4. BEHABITIVES

Behabitives include the notion of reaction to other people's behaviour and fortunes and of attitudes and expressions of attitudes to someone else's past conduct or imminent conduct. There are obvious connexions with both stating or describing what our feelings are and expressing, in the sense of venting our feelings, though behabitives are distinct from both of these.

Examples are:

1. For apologies we have 'apologize'.
2. For thanks we have 'thank'.
3. For sympathy we have 'deplore', 'commiserate', 'compliment', 'condole', 'congratulate', 'felicitate', 'sympathize'.
4. For attitudes we have 'resent', 'don't mind', 'pay tribute', 'criticize', 'grumble about', 'complain of', 'applaud', 'overlook', 'commend', 'deprecate', and the non-exercitive uses of 'blame', 'approve', and 'favour'.
5. For greetings we have 'welcome', 'bid you farewell'.
6. For wishes we have 'bless', 'curse', 'toast', 'drink to', and 'wish' (in its strict performative use).

7. For challenges we have 'dare', 'defy', 'protest', 'challenge'.

In the field of behabitives, besides the usual liability to infelicities, there is a special scope for insincerity.

There are obvious connexions with commissives, for to commend or to support is both to react to behaviour and to commit oneself to a line of conduct. There is also a close connexion with exercitives, for to approve may be an exercise of authority or a reaction to behaviour. Other border line examples are 'recommend', 'overlook', 'protest', 'entreat', and 'challenge'.

5. EXPOSITIVES

Expositives are used in acts of exposition involving the expounding of views, the conducting of arguments, and the clarifying of usages and of references. We have said repeatedly that we may dispute as to whether these are not verdictive, exercitive, behabitive, or commissive acts as well; we may also dispute whether they are not straight descriptions of our feelings, practice, &c., especially sometimes over matters of suiting the action to the words, as when I say 'I turn next to', 'I quote', 'I cite', 'I recapitulate', 'I repeat that', 'I mention that'.

Examples which may well be taken as verdictive are: 'analyse', 'class', 'interpret', which involve exercise of judgment. Examples which may well be taken as exercitive are: 'concede', 'urge', 'argue', 'insist', which involve exertion of influence or exercise of powers.

Examples which may well be taken as commissive are: 'define', 'agree', 'accept', 'maintain', 'support', 'testify', 'swear', which involve assuming an obligation. Examples which may well be taken as behabitive are: 'demur', 'boggle at', which involve adopting an attitude or expressing a feeling.

For good value, I shall give you some lists to indicate the extent of the field. Most central are such examples as 'state', 'affirm', 'deny', 'emphasize', 'illustrate', 'answer'. An enormous number, such as 'question', 'ask', 'deny', &c., seem naturally, but no longer necessarily, to refer to conversational interchange: and all, of course, have reference to the communicational situation.

Here then is a list of expositives:[1]

1.	affirm	3a.	ask
	deny		
	state	4.	testify
	describe		report
	class		swear
	identify		conjecture
			? doubt
2.	remark		? know
	mention		? believe
	? interpose		
		5.	accept
3.	inform		concede
	apprise		withdraw
	tell		agree
	answer		demur to
	rejoin		object to
			adhere to

[1] Austin's layout and numbering are retained here. The general significance of the grouping is obvious but there is no definite key to it in the extant papers. The queries are Austin's. J. O. U.

recognize	conclude by
repudiate	7*a*. interpret
5*a*. correct	distinguish
revise	analyse
	define
6. postulate	7*b*. illustrate
deduce	explain
argue	formulate
neglect	7*c*. mean
? emphasize	refer
	call
7. begin by	understand
turn to	regard as

To sum up, we may say that the verdictive is an exercise of judgment, the exercitive is an assertion of influence or exercising of power, the commissive is an assuming of an obligation or declaring of an intention, the behabitive is the adopting of an attitude, and the expositive is the clarifying of reasons, arguments, and communications.

I have as usual failed to leave enough time in which to say why what I have said is interesting. Just one example then. Philosophers have long been interested in the word 'good' and, quite recently, have begun to take the line of considering how we use it, what we use it to do. It has been suggested, for example, that we use it for expressing approval, for commending, or for grading. But we shall not get really clear about this word 'good' and what we use it to do until, ideally, we have a complete list of those illocutionary acts of which commending, grading, &c., are isolated specimens—until we know how many such acts there are and what are their relationships and inter-connexions. Here, then, is an instance of one possible application of the kind of general theory we have been considering; no doubt there are many others. I have purposely not embroiled the general theory with philosophical problems (some of which are complex enough almost to merit their celebrity); this should not be taken to mean that I am unaware of them. Of course, this is bound to be a little boring and dry to listen to and digest; not nearly so much so as to think and write. Moreover I leave to my readers the real fun of applying it in philosophy.

In these lectures, then, I have been doing two things which I do not altogether like doing. These are:

(1) producing a programme, that is, saying what ought to be done rather than doing something;
(2) lecturing.

However, as against (1), I should very much like to think that I have been sorting out a bit the way things have already begun to go and are going with increasing momentum in some parts of philosophy, rather than proclaiming an individual manifesto. And as against (2), I should certainly like to say that nowhere could, to me, be a nicer place to lecture in than Harvard.

APPENDIX

THE main use of the sets of hearers' lecture notes, the B.B.C. talk on Performatives printed in the *Collected Papers*, the paper delivered at Royaumont under the title 'Performatif—Constatif', and the tape of the lecture given at Gothenberg in October 1959, has been to check the reconstruction of the text initially made independently from Austin's own files of notes. Austin's own notes were found at almost all points to need little supplementation from the secondary sources, being much fuller than any of them. Some characteristic examples have been added from these sources, and also some characteristic phrases at points where Austin's own notes were not in literary form. The main value of the secondary sources has been as a check on order and interpretation at points where the notes are fragmentary.

A list of the more important places at which additions to, and reconstructions of, Austin's text have been made is appended.

Page 7. Lines 9ff. In the notes an extra line has been added after the line ending 'what we need is', which reads: 'in a way, at least draws attention specifically to what we want in certain cases.'

Page 8. By lines 15–16 there is a marginal note which reads: ' "uttering words" not so simple a notion anyway!'

Page 28. The example about George is incomplete in the notes. The text is based mainly on the B.B.C. version.

Page 29. In a separate note there is an addition to point (i) which reads: 'even procedures for bringing oneself under procedures such as "I am playing" May still poss to reject *all*.'

Page 33. Line 3 to the end of the first paragraph is an editorial expansion of very succinct notes.

Page 35. All from the top of the page until, but exclusive of, the final paragraph of the lecture is a composite version from various incomplete versions in notes of differing dates made by Austin.

Page 42. Marginal addition to first line of page reads: 'Restrictions on "thoughts" here?'

Page 44. Marginal addition to last lines of page reads: 'maybe could classify here "moral" obligation X "strict" obligation: but what about threatening not called either!'

Page 52. Marginal note to first line reads:
> to say, presupposes
> saying implies
> what you say entails

Page 52. The final paragraph is an expansion of Austin's notes based mainly on those of Mr. George Pitcher.

Page 64. From this point to the end of the lecture the text is conflated from two sets of notes by Austin made prior to 1955. The 1955 notes are fragmentary at this point.

Page 70. 'Now we can say' to the end of the paragraph is a conjectural expansion of Austin's notes, which read: 'Now we use "how it is to be understood" and "making clear" (and even, conceivably, "state that"): but *not* true or false, not description or report.'

Page 73. Marginal addition by first lines of page reads: 'need criteria for evolution of language.'

Page 73. Marginal addition by paragraph beginning 'The explicit . . .' reads: ' ?misleading: it is *the* device cp. precision.'

Page 90. Marginal addition by line 20 reads: 'and inexplicits do both.'

Page 93. In Austin's notes Lecture VII ends here. It appears from Harvard notes that there the earlier part of Lecture VIII was included in Lecture VII.

Page 95. Marginal note by lines 14–16 reads: 'said ≡ asserted stated.'

Page 103. Marginal note to top of page dated 1958 reads:
Note: (1) All this isn't clear! distinctions etc.
(2) and in all senses relevant ((A) and (B) X (C)) won't all utterances be performative?

Page 105. At line 7 'like implying' is based on Pitcher's notes. Austin has 'Or "imply", is it the same?'

Page 107. Line 29 to the end of the paragraph is added on the basis of secondary sources. It is not in Austin's notes.

Pages 116 and 117. The illustrations to (1) and (2) are added from Pitcher's notes.

Page 118. The paragraph beginning 'So here are ...' is added from Pitcher's notes.

Page 122. Line 3 'A judge ...' to the end of the paragraph is added from Pitcher's notes.

Page 124. The 'iced ink' example, though famous among Austin's pupils, is not in the notes. It is added from many secondary sources.

Page 130. (*a*) and (*b*) are an expansion of very succinct notes based on secondary sources.

Page 137. The notes read literally at the end of the page: 'Contracts often void because objects they're about don't exist—breakdown of reference (total ambiguity or non existence).'

Page 138. Before last sentence of first paragraph of text we have in the notes: '(N.B. Said of course $\frac{\text{never}}{\text{not}}$ state) (Also 'said' has its ambiguities.'

Page 144. The paragraph beginning 'Thirdly . . .' has been expanded on the basis of Messrs. Pitcher's and Demos's notes.

Page 145. In the MS 'were right in' is written over 'right to' at line 15, but 'right to' is not cancelled.

Page 156. In the margin by the comparison with verdictive there is a note that reads: 'Cf. declare war, declare closed, declare state of war exists.'

Page 158. After the paragraph ending 'shall very likely', the notes read: 'Promise that I shall probably'. We suppose that Austin did not intend this as an example of a permissible usage.

Page 160. Note by 'toast' and 'drink to' under 6 reads: 'or suiting action to words.'

Page 163. 'I have as usual failed . . .' to the end is an expansion of Austin's notes based partly on a separate short manuscript note by Austin and confirmed by hearers' notes.

J. O. U.
M. S.

INDEX